AYURVEDIC COOKING FOR SELF-HEALING

A Meal-Time Prayer

अन्नं ब्रह्मा रसो विष्णुः
पक्तोदेवो महेश्वरः ।
एवं ज्ञात्वा तु यो भुन्के
अन्न दोषो न लिप्यते ॥

Annam Brahmā Raso Vishnu,
Pakto Devo Maheśaraḥ
Evam Jñātvā Tu Yo Bhunkte,
Anna Dosho Na Lipyate.

The creative energy in the food is Brahma,
The nourishing energy in the body is Vishnu,
The transformation of food into pure consciousness is Shiva.
If you know this, then any impurities in the food you eat
will never become a part of you.

AYURVEDIC COOKING FOR SELF-HEALING

Second Edition

by

Usha Lad and Dr. Vasant Lad

Albuquerque, New Mexico

The Ayurvedic Press, Albuquerque 87112

This book is printed on acid-free, FSC® certified paper.
ISBN-13: 978-1-883725-05-1

> Although the information contained in this book is based on Ayurvedic principles practiced for thousands of years, it should not be taken or construed as standard medical treatment. For any medical condition, always consult with a qualified physician.

Cover Photos: The Lad Family & friends. Art work: drawn by Vasant Lad.
Cover Design: Laura Humphreys
The authors lovingly acknowledge the support and help of everyone at the Ayurvedic Institute in Albuquerque.

Library of Congress Cataloging-in-Publication Data

Lad, Vasant, 1943-
　　Ayurvedic Cooking for Self-Healing / by Usha and Vasant Lad.
　　　　254 p.: ill. ; 23 cm.
Includes bibliographical references (p. 243) and index.
　　ISBN: 9781883725051
　1. Vegetarian cookery. 2. Cookery, Indic. 3. Medicine, Ayurvedic.
I. Title.
　　RM236 .L33 1997
　　641.5/636 21
                                                        97-070608

For more information on Ayurveda contact:
The Ayurvedic Institute, 11311 Menaul Blvd NE, Albuquerque, NM 87112
Phone (505) 291-9698 • Ayurveda.com.

Dedication

To our most loving children, Aparna and Pranav

TABLE OF CONTENTS

Lord Ganesha

ॐ गँ गणपतये नमः ।

Salutation to the Lord Ganesha who is the seed of wisdom and light.
(translation of Sutra)

Ganesha is the son of Shiva and Parvati.
He is the first Lord to be worshipped at the beginning of any auspicious work.
He removes obstacles and brings success, fulfillment and great joy to the life of every human being.
Cooking is a very auspicious work, which brings nourishment, health and fulfillment to both the cook and the guest.
One should worship Ganesha before cooking and eating.
He is the Lord of Plenty who carries a bowl, full of the food of Bliss.

FOREWORD

Some of the fondest memories of my years of Ayurvedic study in India involve the Lad family. No sooner did I meet Dr. Vasant Lad in January 1974 than he invited me home for dinner, a dinner which inaugurated a veritable procession of future meals. When classes were in session at Pune's Tilak Ayurveda Mahavidyalaya, Dr. Lad frequently would insist that I share his lunch and soon I was consuming many of my meals in the Lad home, a practice which continued during most of the six years I spent at the college. Whenever I would arrive at her door, Usha Tai (Mrs. Lad) would offer me some freshly-prepared tidbit. If the cupboard was temporarily bare, apologetically she would begin to whip something up from scratch, no matter how vociferously I might protest. Even when I was living on only milk and fruits, a glass of milk was always waiting for me, day or night.

Like many Indians, Usha Tai genuinely loves to cook for guests, because every guest, indeed every living being, bears the spark of divinity. That I had arrived in her home meant that I should be fed, not as some grudging obligation but from the love of cooking and feeding. Every morsel fed to that visiting incarnation of God is a morsel fed back to the Creator as an offering of gratitude for Nature's bounty; and since the scriptures remind us that "food is indeed God," to feed the hungry is to serve God to God. Food creates the *rasa*, that juicy nutritional essence which nourishes the body's hungry tissues and pleases and satisfies the mind and the senses. This nourishment and satisfaction are the blessings that Annapurna, the goddess of food, has awarded to all sentient beings, and the Lads have believed always in sharing their blessings freely.

As I watched time pass in the Lads' kitchen, I had ample occasion to see first hand the sort of attention Usha Tai lavished on the food she prepared. I watched her shop and select, grind and chop, sauté and boil, and imbibed that rhythm of food preparation which makes the victuals begin to cook themselves as soon as they enter the pot. Her culinary preparations were a practical demonstration of what I was being taught theoretically in the college, namely that the standard linear logic that serves the physical sciences so well is of little use when it comes to the arts of living, such as medicine and cookery. Only when you gain a real feel for food, which happens when Annapurna begins to possess you, can you know what cuisine can really mean.

On Sundays, when the hospital's outpatient departments were closed and the relative quiet permitted Dr. Lad to sally forth himself on grocery expeditions, I would accompany him to learn more about the indications of a certain vegetable, or about the type of people who would do best with a particular fruit. Sometimes we would purchase herbs and parboil them into potions, a dramatic demonstration of the rule that a good *vaidya* (Ayurvedic physician) must also be a good cook. After months and months of such informal preparations, I myself then began to cook under the watchful gaze of my mentor Vimalananda and, before long, I added the pleasure of feeding others to the pleasure of being fed, all thanks to my sojourn with the Lads.

I know from personal experience how consistently the Lad family has followed an Ayurvedic lifestyle over the twenty years that I have known them, and so I acceded with great pleasure to Usha Tai's request to write the introduction to her book on Ayurvedic cooking. The good Ayurvedic teachers are those like Dr. Lad who have learned and who have performed, and the good cooks are those like Usha Tai who have sweated and have served. May this book help all those who are sincerely willing to learn the true meaning of feeding and being fed that they may gain a new awareness of what food can mean to a life well lived.

Dr. Robert E. Svoboda
Dipavali, 1993

PREFACE

During and after my internship, I worked as a house physician in the departments of medicine, surgery, gynecology and pediatrics at the Ayurvedic Hospital in Pune. At that time I observed over and over again how the correct diet, combined with proper herbal medicine and lifestyle, can play a vital role in healing. I became increasingly aware that illness provides an "invitation" to change one's habitual patterns related to thinking, feeling and feeding ourselves properly.

My outlook began to move from the commonly used labels for an illness, such as "this is influenza or that is a virus," to the inner sense of how that illness manifested according to basic Ayurvedic theories. I incorporated a deeper and subtler understanding of the interplay of the *doshas* in health and disease and of how nature's gentle source of healing with herbs and food can bring healing and balance. As my awareness grew about the role of food as medicine, I observed that many health problems seemed intertwined with the stresses of daily life. These include worries about one's job or money, tension and even the stress created by eating the wrong kinds of food and improper food combining.

In the last twenty years I have seen many problems, sometimes culminating in serious illness, that were the result of poor food choices and ignorance of the art of proper cooking for oneself and for the family. While working in the *panchakarma* department at the hospital, I saw the impressive effects of this cleansing program administered in conjunction with proper diet, which is usually a mono-fast on a single food. This also taught me that food is medicine when rightly used.

In this book you will find simple, practical approaches to food and specific recipes from the Ayurvedic art of cooking to help restore the body's healthful balance. Though there is much helpful information within these covers, this book is not proposed as a treatment plan for any disease. This, of course, you must obtain from your own doctor.

Much of the information here can be classified best as the "intuitive science of life." It comes from my own practical clinical experience, founded on the basic principles built from thousands of years of Ayurvedic medicine. This is not a "scientific" method, as the term is used in Western medicine, but the information carefully gathered from centuries of day-to-day experience.

For instance, sour fruits, fermented food and hot spices provoke *pitta* and can cause acid indigestion and heartburn. Black beans and pinto beans aggravate *vata*, can create gas and can lead to bloating and discomfort. Yogurt, cheese and cold drinks aggravate *kapha* and may lead to cold, cough and congestion. This book will help you to develop a good understanding of the wise and practical Ayurvedic approach to food and health.

I hope you will find that the suggestions in this book become a vital part of your own self-healing. The golden keys to health lie in getting in touch with your inner self and in seeing the process of healing as a useful means of learning about your own unique needs.

I met my wife Usha at the Ayurvedic Hospital in Pune where she was a student of Ayurvedic nursing. After we were married, Usha began using her knowledge and love of Ayurveda as her guiding light in preparing our meals. She always brings great love and respect to every stage of food preparation, and she cooks each meal with all of her heart.

By calling this book *Ayurvedic Cooking For Self-Healing*, my wish is that you will discover a creative program for better health for yourself and your family. These recipes and healing ways are meant to enter into your life as a natural method of healing without any side effects or reactions. Keeping you healthy and balanced in all seasons is the goal of this practical "guidebook" about food.

Enjoy your Ayurvedic cooking for health, happiness and the healing of family and friends.

God bless you with love and light.

Dr. Vasant Lad
Albuquerque
March 1994

AN INTRODUCTION TO AYURVEDIC COOKING

There are many varieties of cookbooks available in bookstores today that represent a wide array of different eating habits and concepts of nutrition, some very traditional and others very modern or resulting from short-lived fads. Health-conscious people are interested in the role good nourishment can play in their healing and in their health. It is indeed true that we are what we eat.

Ayurveda, the ancient medical system of India, encompasses the healing of body, mind and spirit through diet, lifestyle and rejuvenation. Cleansing programs and medicinal herbs accompany these procedures. This art of wholistic healing teaches that food and diet can make a vital contribution to continuous good health. Ayurveda can provide much insight about which foods will suit and balance each individual, how to prepare and cook these foods properly and how to avoid combinations that will create toxins in the body.

The main purpose of this book is to help you choose a suitable diet for balance, harmony and health in your life, based on Ayurvedic principles. It also introduces simple, tasty recipes that can become part of one's regular diet, as well as a selection that can be used to help various health conditions. But first some understanding of Ayurveda is necessary to provide the perspective on why and how changing one's food habits can have such a profound effect on health and well-being.

The Ayurvedic science of food and diet is vast and comprehensive, and influences every aspect of one's life. Ayurveda is the eternal science of life. The tradition of Ayurveda extends back more than five thousand years and has been practiced continuously to the present day. Although India has seen many different rulers and aggressors, it has never lost its integrity and essential nature as evidenced by Ayurveda's ancient tradition and continuity.

In 900 B.C., three magnificent scholars, Charak, Sushruta and Vagbhata, gave this oral tradition a new and wonderful form by writing down the principles of Ayurveda. Today, their textbooks are still used by students, practitioners and all Ayurvedic medical schools and colleges throughout India.

Many different schools of healing therapy popular today, such as massage, physiotherapy, nutrition, herbal remedies, plastic surgery, psychiatry, polarity, kinesiology, shiatsu, *mantra*, meditation, color and gem therapy, have their roots firmly planted in Ayurvedic philosophy. In the truest sense, Ayurveda is the mother of all healing systems.

In order to understand how to choose food according to your needs and body type and to learn the basic Ayurvedic ways of cooking, it is essential to perceive the central working principles of Ayurveda.

Chapter 1

YOUR INDIVIDUAL CONSTITUTION

The concept of constitution (*prakruti* in Sanskrit) is the main framework and the very heart of Ayurveda. Ayurveda teaches that there are three basic *doshas*—called *vata, pitta* and *kapha*—and that every human being has some combination of these principles in his or her makeup. Your own unique *prakruti* is the clue or the map to discovering the foods and lifestyle that will balance you. Without understanding the three *doshas* or *tridosha*, one cannot fully realize the hidden secrets of ancient Ayurvedic cooking.

The Elements

Tridoshas are dynamic principles that govern the body, mind and consciousness. They are subject to a person's genetic makeup and emotional and mental paradigms, as well as any imbalances. Let us begin to comprehend the view of the *tridoshas* by briefly learning about the five basic elements of our planet.

The human body and, indeed, the entire world are composed of the same fundamental principles: Space, Air, Fire, Water and Earth. All organic and inorganic substances are made up of combinations of these ingredients. Much of the physical universe is the interaction of these five elements.

All-pervading Space serves as the common factor or "home" for all objects in the universe. Air is active, mobile, dry and the vital life-force, or *prana*, essential for all living creatures. Without Air, life is not possible on this, or any, planet. Fire governs digestion, absorption and assimilation in the living organism as well as the flowering, ripening and decay of plants. The sun—the eye of heaven, the lamp of day—is the central source of heat energy. The life-sustaining, liquid, cool element is Water. It maintains electrolyte balance, nourishes plants and animals and sustains the environment. The solid, dense and hard element is Earth, the firm ground for global life. It cradles and holds all living creatures of the planet, giving them food and shelter.

These five elements normally support life and maintain harmony in the world but, when they are out of balance, can cause discomfort and threaten life. The predominance of each element, by its very nature, changes continuously, modifying temperature, humidity, time and seasons. People must strive to accommodate these changes for sheer survival. Having intelligence, human beings use these same elements against one another in order to create optimum environmental conditions. For example, they build brick (Earth element) houses to protect themselves from changes in air, heat and water.

All the elements are present in each individual, but the proportions and combinations vary from person to person. Keeping one's individual qualitative and quantitative balance of these five basic elements is responsible for perfect health. When your own unique combination of the elements is maintained, your health is good. But when the combination is upset, disease may result. For instance, an increased Earth component can result in obesity, increased Water can lead to edema or increased Fire can cause fever, ulcers and any burning sensations such as heartburn, conjunctivitis or burning urination. Subtle changes in the mental faculties may also appear when the equilibrium is upset, such as an aggravation of Air causing fear and anxiety, of Fire leading to anger and hate, and of Earth bringing depression and dullness.

Tridosha — Vata, Pitta and Kapha

Ancient Ayurveda might have considered classifying human beings into five body types based upon the predominant element. But as Space is essentially inert and Earth is the solid, supporting foundation of creation, these two elements are considered mostly passive. The active, mobile and changing elements are Air, Fire and Water.

Ayurveda incorporates these three active elements into the principle of tridosha.

VATA represents Air and Space.

PITTA is the Fire along with Water.

KAPHA is Water and Earth.

Vata, pitta and kapha are the very foundation of Ayurveda. The concept of the humors—bile, blood and phlegm—found in European medicine of the past is likely just one of the many offsprings of Ayurveda.

At the moment of conception, each person's combination and proportions of vata, pitta and kapha are determined according to the genetics, diet, lifestyle and emotions of the parents. A few fortunate individuals are born with a balanced constitution, where all three doshas are equal in quality and quantity. These people are blessed with good health and excellent digestion. However, the majority of people will have one or two doshas prominent. With the proper diet and lifestyle, they can achieve optimum health.

Most people have a prakruti of one of seven combinations of vata, pitta and kapha. For instance, a person might be mostly kapha with a secondary characteristic of pitta and a small amount of vata. In Ayurveda this would be written V1 P2 K3. A person might be equally pitta and vata with a small amount of kapha. This would be written this V3 P3 K1. The numbers serve to suggest the relative proportions of each dosha.

Prakruti and Vikruti

The combination of the three doshas, which is set at conception, is called prakruti. The prakruti does not change during one's lifetime, except in very rare cases. There is also a constitution "of the moment" reflecting one's current state of health called *vikruti*. In a person of excellent health, the proportions of vikruti will be the same as prakruti. But more likely there will be a difference, for vikruti reflects any aspects of diet, lifestyle, emotions, age, environment, etc. that are not in harmony with one's prakruti. This difference can be established by an Ayurvedic physician through a variety of procedures such as taking a life history, analyzing the face and tongue, and taking the pulse. It is this difference between prakruti and vikruti that provides the Ayurvedic physician with precise information to formulate a program for restoring health.

Determining Your Constitution

There are steps you can take toward restoring or improving your health through learning about your constitution. The best way to find out your own prakruti and vikruti is to use the services of an Ayurvedic physician. But if this is not possible, you can make a reasonable guess at determining these by filling in the "Your Constitution" chart in the Appendix at the back of this book.

Before turning to the chart, it is helpful to be familiar with the qualities of each dosha. No matter what your constitution turns out to be, it is possible to achieve optimum health through proper diet, cooking methods, lifestyle and an attitude that specifically suits you.

Characteristics of the Vata Individual

The Sanskrit term vata is derived from the verb "va," meaning to carry or move. So vata is the principle of mobility that regulates all activity in the body, from how many thoughts one might have in a minute to how efficiently food moves through the intestines. The vata quality is responsible for joy, happiness, creativity, speech, sneezing and elimination, to name just a few functions. Vata is in charge of the vital life essence, oxygen or prana. Thus when vata leaves the body, life ceases.

Vata has the qualities or attributes of dry, light, cold, rough, subtle, mobile and clear, with an astringent taste. How these qualities translate into the makeup of the vata individual is shown in the chart on the next page.

This combination of qualities can be responsible for both physical characteristics and behavioral patterns in vata persons. Physically they have a light, flexible body, big, protruding teeth and may have sucked their fingers or thumb. They have small, recessed, dry eyes. With irregular appetite and thirst, they often experience digestive and malabsorption problems. V ⅛tas tend to be delicate in health, so may have few or no children.

In their behavior, vata individuals are easily excited. Indeed, they are alert and quick to act without much thinking. So they may give a wrong answer, but with great confidence. Though they are blessed by a distinguished power of imagination, they love daydreaming. They are quite loving people, but they may love someone out of fear or loneliness. Fears of darkness, heights and enclosed spaces are not uncommon in vata individuals. Their faith is flexible and ready to change, but the change does not necessarily stay long. *Vātas* love change. This is why they change furniture, place or town often, to keep from feeling bored. They do not like sitting idle, they love constant action. Not doing anything is a punishment for them. Due to their active nature, they make good money, but they spend it on trifles and have difficulty saving.

THE ATTRIBUTES OF THE VATA INDIVIDUAL

Attributes	Manifestations In The Body
Dry	dry skin, hair, lips, tongue; dry colon, tending toward constipation; hoarse voice
Light	light muscles, bones, thin body frame, light scanty sleep; underweight
Cold	cold hands, feet, poor circulation; hates cold and loves hot; stiffness of muscles
Rough	rough, cracked skin, nails, hair, teeth, hands and feet; cracking joints
Subtle	subtle fear, anxiety, insecurity; fine goose-pimples; minute muscle twitching, fine tremors
Mobile	fast walking, talking, doing many things at a time; restless eyes, eyebrows, hands, feet; unstable joints; many dreams; loves travelling but does not stay at one place; swinging moods, shaky faith, scattered mind
Clear	clairvoyant; understands and forgets immediately; clear, empty mind, experiences void and loneliness
Astringent	dry choking sensation in the throat; gets hiccoughs, burping; loves oily, mushy soups; craving for sweet, sour and salty tastes
Brownish-black	Dark complexion; dark hair and eyes; color of vata ama, e.g., dark coated tongue

Characteristics of the Pitta Individual

The word pitta is derived from the Sanskrit word "tapa," meaning to heat. Pitta represents the Fire principle in the body. Literally everything that enters the body must be digested or "cooked," from the sight of a new moon to the wild strawberry popped into the mouth. Some foods, like rice, need external cooking as well before the body fire can begin digestion. Along with the gastric fire, pitta is the enzymes and amino acids that play a major role in metabolism.

Just a few of pitta's responsibilities are regulating body heat through chemical transformation of food, giving one an appetite, vitality, learning and understanding. Out-of-balance pitta can cause anger, hate and criticism to surface.

Pitta is hot, sharp, light, oily, liquid and spreading in nature. It is sour, bitter, pungent to the taste and has a fleshy smell. It is associated with the colors red and yellow. These qualities are revealed in the body of the pitta person, as shown in the chart on the next page.

By virtue of the attributes listed in the table at right, pitta people have a moderately delicate body with a medium frame and weight. They seldom gain or lose much weight. They may have sharp, yellowish teeth with soft and, at times, bleeding gums. Their eyes are bright but sensitive to light. With strong appetite and thirst, they tend to like hot and spice foods.

Pittas have great learning, understanding and concentrating abilities. With excellent organizing and leadership capacity, they are highly disciplined. They are blessed with wisdom, which is reflected by glowing baldness. (So much wisdom indeed that it "burns" off their hair!) Pitta individuals never yield an inch from their principles, which sometimes leads to fanaticism. As a matter of fact, they can be judgmental, critical and perfectionistic, so they tend to become angry easily. They love noble professions, and they often make big money to spend on luxurious items. They like perfumes and jewelry. They may not have a strong sex drive. Overall, pitta constitution is endowed with moderate strength, average spiritual and material knowledge, wealth and lifespan.

THE ATTRIBUTES OF THE PITTA INDIVIDUAL

Attributes	*Manifestations In The Body*
Hot	good digestive fire; strong appetite; body temperature tends to be higher than average; hates heat; gray hair with receding hair line or baldness; soft brown hair on the body and face
Sharp	sharp teeth, distinct eyes, pointed nose, heart-shaped face, tapering chin; good absorption and digestion; sharp memory and understanding; intolerance of hard work; irritable; probing mind
Light	light/medium body frame; does not tolerate bright light; fair shiny skin, bright eyes
Liquid	loose liquid stools; soft delicate muscles; excess urine, sweat and thirst
Spreading (mobile)	*pitta* spreads as rash, acne, or inflammation all over the body or on affected areas; pitta subjects want to spread their name and fame all over the country
Oily	soft oily skin, hair, feces; may not digest deep-fried food (which can cause headache)
Sour	sour acid stomach, acidic pH; sensitive teeth; excess salivation
Pungent	heartburn, burning sensations in general; strong feelings of anger and hate
Bitter	bitter taste in the mouth, nausea, vomiting; repulsion toward bitter taste; cynical
Fleshy smell	fetid smell under armpits, mouth, soles of feet; socks smell
Red	red flushed skin, eyes, cheeks and nose; red color aggravates *pitta*; does not tolerate heat and sunlight; color of pitta without ama
Yellow	yellow eyes, skin, urine and feces; may lead to jaundice, over production of bile; yellow color increases pitta; pale yellow is normal pitta but dark yellow is color of pitta ama

Characteristics of the Kapha Individual

The phrase kapha comes from two Sanskrit roots, "ka" meaning water and "pha" meaning to flourish. Kapha's nature is also Earth, so Earth and Water give kapha its definitive qualities. Kapha comprises all our cells, tissues and organs. Kapha molecules tend to stick together to form compact masses and give the body a chubby shape. Lubrication of joints and organs, strong muscles and bones, cellular secretions and memory retention are all part of kapha's water duties.

Water and Earth give kapha the qualities of heavy, slow, cool, oily, damp, smooth, dense, soft, static, viscous and cloudy. It is white in color and has a sweet and salty taste. The presentation of these qualities in the kapha constitution is in the table on the following page.

The above qualities give a strong and healthy body, big, beautiful eyes, healthy teeth and thick, curly hair to people of kapha constitution. They have thick, smooth, oily and hairy skin. Kaphas have a steady appetite and thirst, but slow digestion and metabolism. This often results in weight gain, which they have great difficulty in shedding. At times, cravings for sweet and salt lead to water retention. They love eating, sitting, doing nothing and sleeping for a long time.

Kapha people are blessed with a deep, stable faith, with love and compassion and a calm, steady mind. They have a good memory, a deep melodious voice and a monotonous pattern of speech. A kapha person makes and saves money. Extravagances may be spending a little amount on cheese, candy and cakes. An unbalanced kapha suffers from greed, attachment, ignorance and laziness. All in all, the kapha individual is endowed with excellent strength, knowledge, peace, love and longevity, due to a strong constitution.

THE ATTRIBUTES OF THE KAPHA INDIVIDUAL

Attributes	Manifestations In The Body
Heavy	heavy bones, muscles, large body frame; tends to be overweight; grounded; deep heavy voice
Slow/Dull	slow walk, talk; slow digestion, metabolism; sluggish gestures
Cool (Cold)	cold clammy skin; steady appetite and thirst with slow metabolism and digestion; repeated cold, congestion and cough; desire for sweets

Attributes	*Manifestations In The Body*
Oily	oily skin, hair and feces; lubricated, unctuous joints and other organs
Liquid	excess salivation; congestion in the chest, sinuses, throat and head
Slimy/Smooth	smooth skin; smoothness of organs; smooth, gentle mind; calm nature
Dense	dense pad of fat; thick skin, hair, nail and feces; plump rounded organs; firmness and solidity of muscles; compact, condensed tissues
Soft	soft pleasing look; love, care, compassion, kindness, and forgiveness
Static	loves sitting, sleeping and doing nothing
Sticky	viscous, cohesive quality causes compactness, firmness of joints and organs; loves to hug; is deeply attached in love and relationships
Cloudy	in early morning mind is cloudy and foggy; often desires coffee as a stimulant to start the day
Hard	firm muscles; strength; rigid attitude
Gross	causes obstruction; obesity
Sweet	the anabolic action of sweet taste stimulates sperm formation increasing quantity of semen; abnormal function may cause craving for sweets
Salty	helps digestion and growth, gives energy; maintains osmotic condition; abnormal function may create craving for salt, water retention
White	pale complexion; white mucous; white coating on tongue; color of kapha ama

VATA TEA
(Recipe — page 180)

Chapter 2

FACTORS THAT AFFECT OUR HEALTH

Ayurveda is a way of healing and a way of life that always takes into consideration the whole person. According to the teachings of Ayurveda, every aspect of life contributes to overall health. Poor health seldom has a simple or single cause. This chapter will cover just a few of the things that may affect one's well-being. Some factors will respond to changes, like diet, and some are beyond individual control, like the weather. With the latter, there are actions that can be taken to reduce or eliminate the impact. Of course, it is not possible or wise to try to change everything at once. Ayurvedic literature states slow and steady is the best route to successful change. Most people find that diet is the best place to begin an Ayurvedic lifestyle.

The Doshas

One's sense of well-being reflects the inner state of health. Good health is the maintenance of one's unique combination of the doshas, a balanced condition of *agni*, of the seven body tissues, of the three waste systems (urine, sweat and feces), as well as balance in the mind, senses and consciousness. It is equally important to one's well-being to have love, happiness and clarity in daily living.

Doshic imbalance governs internal biochemical changes that will eventually lead to either high or low metabolism.

Pitta dosha governs all physical and biochemical changes that take place within the body. Through this process foodstuffs are transformed into energy, heat and vitality. Pitta performs these functions throughout one's life, but is especially prominent during the adult years. All these activities of pitta depend upon "digestive fire" or agni. Poor agni means poor health.

Wrong diet such as hot spicy foods, wrong lifestyle such as living in a hot climate and repressed emotions can alter the normal function of pitta.

Anabolism is the process of building up the body. It is the repair, growth and creation of new cells. This process is managed by kapha and is most active in the baby, child and teen years. *Kapha dosha* can be disturbed by excessive intake of dairy, cold and oily foods.

Catabolism is the destructive, but necessary, stage of metabolism. Larger molecules are broken down into smaller ones. This molecular death is governed by *vata dosha* and is most active in old age. Repeated intake of vata-provoking food, such as salads and popcorn, and over-exercising can escalate vata and disturb health.

Improper Eating Habits

1. Overeating
2. Eating soon after a full meal
3. Too much water or no water during a meal
4. Drinking very chilled water during a meal or, indeed, anytime
5. Eating when constipated
6. Eating at the wrong time of day—either too early or too late
7. Eating too much heavy food or too little light food
8. Drinking fruit juice or eating fruit with a meal
9. Eating without real hunger
10. Emotional eating
11. Eating incompatible food combinations
12. Snacking in between meals

Time of Day and Time of Season

The body's biological clock is regulated by the doshas. The time of maximum activity of kapha is during early morning and early evening, 6 to 10 am and 6 to 10 pm. The pitta period is during midday and midnight, 10 am to 2 pm and 10 pm to 2 am, while vata hours are dawn and dusk, 2 to 6 am and 2 to 6 pm. Thus a pitta-type disease, like ulcers, may cause the most discomfort late at night in the pitta time of the bio-clock. The reverse is also true, in the sense that experiencing a sharp pain in the stomach region late at night may signify ulcers or another pitta-type aggravation.

After food is ingested, it passes through various stages of digestion, each one involving a specific dosha. To digest one major meal takes 6 to 8 hours. For approximately two-and-a-half hours after eating food, the dominant dosha is kapha, which is associated with the stomach. Roughly two-and-a-half hours later, pitta dosha is dominant. This period and dosha are associated with the small intestine, where bile and intestinal enzymes are at work. Ultimately, the digestion is completed in the colon, the predominant site of vata, where absorption and elimination occur. This stage is a time of vata domination. Gas, a quality of vata, will often occur here if food is not properly digested.

The seasons have attributes much like the three doshas and can cause aggravation and imbalance. For instance, the summer is hot, sharp and bright which provokes pitta. So pitta diseases like sunburn, hot flashes, exhaustion, acne and diarrhea may occur. Psychologically, people may respond to trifles with anger and hate.

Autumn is dry, light, cold, clear and windy, all aggravating qualities to vata dosha. Aches and pains in the joints and muscles may materialize, and the mind may become fearful, anxious and lonely.

The heavy, cold, dampness of winter can provoke kapha, leading to cough, cold and sinus congestion. Attachment and greed may develop in the mind when kapha is aggravated.

The watery quality of spring also provokes kapha and some people will tend to have spring colds, allergies and respiratory ailments at this time.

The change from one season to another may require shifting one's diet for a period of time to restore balance.

Getting The Right Amount of Exercise

Exercise, too, should be in harmony with the specific constitution. Kapha individuals can perform the most strenuous exercise, pitta a medium amount and vata the gentlest. Aerobics, swimming, fast walking and biking are all good exercise for pitta and kapha, but not for vata. Vata tends to love jumping and jogging, but exercises like yoga, stretching and T'ai Chi are better choices. For people with serious vata and pitta disorders and for those whose age is over 80 or under 10, exercise should be very gentle. Walking is probably the best exercise of all for any constitution.

Even for a healthy individual, Ayurveda suggests a workout that is one-half of one's capacity, just until sweat appears on the forehead, under the arms and along the spinal column. This amount of exercise stimulates gastric fire, improves digestion and relieves constipation, as well as inducing relaxation and sound sleep. Sweating helps to eliminate toxins, reduce fat and make you feel good. Over-exercising may cause dehydration and breathlessness, even chest pain and muscle aches, eventually leading to arthritis, sciatica or heart conditions.

Choosing a Balanced Lifestyle

Lifestyle has its own definite rhythm in each person's life. Waking too early or late, irregular food habits, staying up late, job stress, untimely bowel movements and suppression of natural urges are a few habits that can unsettle one. Regularity in sleeping, waking, eating and elimination, indeed following a daily routine, brings discipline and helps to maintain the integrity of the *doshas* and good health.

Ayurveda has some definite suggestions about the role of sex in one's life. Sexual activity should be avoided after heavy meals, during hunger or in anger, for this could be detrimental to health. The right amount and right time is important. *Vata* should not make love more than once or, at most, twice a month, *pitta* once every two weeks and *kapha* two to three times a week. The best time for making love is between 10 and 11 PM. Too frequent lovemaking reduces *ojas*, the vital energy, and leaves the person weak and open to disease. *Ojas* should be restored after sexual activity through massage and nourishing drinks, such as almond milk.

Relationships and Emotions

Daily life is relationships, both the relationships we have with one another and the one we have with ourselves. Ideally, clarity, compassion and love should characterize these relationships. It is often easier to love and respect others than one's self. Relationships are mirrors to use for self-learning, inquiry and investigation. Through that very learning, radical transformation of one's life can take place. If our relationships are unclear, confusion and conflict will affect our well-being.

Emotions, such as anger, fear or anxiety, arise from reactions to our daily relationships. These reactions appear due to inattention to the moment. Each person needs to pay total attention to his or her thoughts, feelings and emotions. If one doesn't, these emotions will be undigested and just as capable of poisoning the body as bad food combinations. Each emotion is a biochemical response to a challenge and may provoke the doshas. Fear and anxiety will provoke vata, anger and hate will upset pitta and attachment and greed will aggravate kapha.

Meditation and Well-Being

Meditation plays a most important part in daily life and is a powerful tool to help maintain health. While the dictionary says that the term meditation means to think, to ponder, to go through and examine, this definition does not impart the profound meaning of the word. Mediation is an action of clear perception, an observation with total awareness and without any conclusion, judgment or criticism. Meditation demands that you be utterly one with the moment. In this oneness, there is radical change in one's psyche. In this moment-to-moment awareness, there is a cleansing of the body, mind and consciousness. This cleansing will bring one to that state of peace which is joy, bliss and enlightenment. At that point, life becomes a movement of spontaneous meditation.

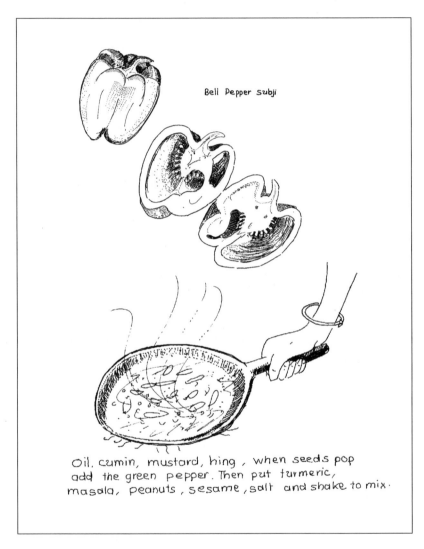

Bell Pepper Subji

Oil, cumin, mustard, hing, when seeds pop add the green pepper. Then put turmeric, masala, peanuts, sesame, salt and shake to mix.

BELL PEPPER SUBJI
(Recipe — page 100)

Chapter 3

TASTE AND DIGESTION

Ayurveda regards food in a very unique and integrated way. Understanding some of these principles will help one to recognize the foods that will keep the *doshas* in balance.

Qualities of Food

In an earlier chapter, it was shown that each dosha has certain attributes or qualities, such as dry, hot or heavy. The following is a chart showing the basic qualities that apply equally to a food item or a specific dosha.

THE 20 BASIC ATTRIBUTES OR QUALITIES

Heavy	Light	Cold	Hot
Oily	Dry	Slow	Sharp
Stable	Mobile	Soft	Hard
Slimy	Rough	Dense	Liquid
Gross	Subtle	Cloudy	Clear

In the same way as the doshas, each kind of food is made up of certain qualities; for example, popcorn is light and dry and cheese is heavy and slow.

These qualities have a direct effect on how the body accepts and digests a particular food. Even one's emotional outlook can be directly affected, such as the mind feeling sharp and irritable after eating hot chili peppers.

In general, when the qualities of a food are similar to the qualities of a *dosha*, this will tend to be aggravating to that *dosha*, as when a *vata* (dry) person eats popcorn (dry). Opposite qualities, a *pitta* (Fire) person drinking mint tea (cooling), tend to be calming. This fundamental principle can help you select the right foods for you.

EXAMPLES OF THE ATTRIBUTES OF CERTAIN FOODS

Heavy	cheese, meat, beans
Light	rice, popcorn, sprouts, caffeine
Cold	ice cream, chilled milk, mint
Hot	chili pepper, alcohol, tobacco
Oily	cheese, avocado, olive oil, coconut
Dry	millet, rye, dry cereal
Slow	meat, yogurt
Sharp	onions, garlic
Stable	*ghee*, warm milk
Mobile	alcohol, sprouts, popcorn

The Concepts of *Rasa, Virya, Vipaka* and *Prabhav*

According to Ayurvedic philosophy, the moon is the deity of water. Water in the atmosphere in its pure form is cold, light, clear and without any taste. This water eventually falls to the ground, interacts with the other elements and enters the plants. This nectar of the moon yields and creates various tastes in each plant. Water, then, is the mother of all tastes. Tastes are perceived by the tongue, our sense organ of Water. A dry tongue cannot taste accurately.

Each food substance, each medicinal herb, has a specific taste. The moment a substance touches the tongue, the first experience is the taste. Taste is a very important quality and has a direct effect on bodily doshas. Ayurveda recognizes six basic tastes—sweet, sour, salty, bitter, pungent and astringent.

All these tastes are present in the plasma. Every food is made up of some combination of the five basic elements, and so these elements are present in the six tastes. The unique union of elements actually gives food its taste. The relationships between the elements and the tastes are given in the chart below.

HOW TASTE RELATES TO THE ELEMENTS

TASTES	ELEMENTS
Sweet	Earth + Water
Sour	Earth + Fire
Salty	Water + Fire
Pungent	Air + Fire
Bitter	Air + Space
Astringent	Air + Earth

The Fire and Air elements are light and tend to move upward, hence the tastes containing these elements also move up and heat the upper parts of the body, producing lightness. Conversely, the Earth and Water elements are heavy and move downward, so the sweet taste cools the lower part, the urinary passage, and can produce heaviness in the body.

THE CONNECTION OF THE ELEMENTS AND FOODS

Earth   Wheat, rice. Meat. Mushrooms, root vegetables and beans. Hard, dried fruits. Sesame, sunflower and pumpkin seeds. Almonds, cashews and walnuts. Salts and minerals.

Water   Milk and dairy products. Juicy fruits such as plums, watermelon, grapes, cantaloupe, oranges, papaya and peaches. Coconut water. Juicy vegetables such as cucumbers, zucchini and tomatoes. Salts.

Fire   Spices like hot peppers, black pepper, chili pepper, cinnamon, cloves, cardamom, turmeric, ginger, asafoetida (hing), garlic and onions. Sour fruits such as pineapple, lemons and some oranges. Berries like cranberries. Alcohol. Tobacco.

Air   Substances which produce gas such as dried fruits and raw vegetables. Rough vegetables like broccoli, cabbages and sprouts. Nightshades like potatoes, tomatoes and eggplants. Some beans like black beans, pinto beans and chickpeas.

Space   Intoxicating, hypnotic and narcotic drugs such as alcohol, marijuana, LSD, cocaine and tobacco.

Rasa and the Action of Taste

Every food's unique combination of attributes will influence its taste and the action it causes in the body. The concept of taste (*rasa*), action (*virya*) and post-digestive effect (*vipaka*) will further one's understanding of the basic principles of Ayurvedic cooking and healing.

Sweet The sweet taste is present in foods such as sugar, milk, rice, wheat, dates, maple syrup and licorice. Earth and Water are the elements that make up the sweet taste. The qualities are usually oily, cooling and heavy. The sweet taste increases the vital essence of life. When used moderately, it is wholesome to the body and anabolic in action, promoting the growth of plasma, blood, muscles, fat, bones, marrow and reproductive fluids. Proper use gives strength and longevity. It encourages the senses, improves complexion, promotes healthy skin and hair and a good voice. Sweet taste can relieve thirst, burning sensations and be invigorating. It can bring about stability and heal emaciation.

In spite of all these good qualities, excessive use can produce many disorders in all the doshas. sweet foods especially aggravate kapha and cause cold, cough, congestion, heaviness, loss of appetite, laziness and obesity. They may also cause abnormal muscle growth, lymphatic congestion, tumors, edema and diabetes.

Sour   Sour taste is found in foods like citrus fruits, sour cream, yogurt, vinegar, cheese, lemon, unripe mango, green grapes and fermented food. Sour substances are liquid, light, heating, oily in nature and anabolic in action. When used in moderation, they are refreshing and delicious to the taste, stimulate appetite, improve digestion, energize the body, nourish the heart, enlighten the mind and cause salivation.

If one uses the sour taste in excess, it can cause sensitive teeth, excessive thirst, quick, reflexive closure of eyes, hyperacidity, heartburn, acid indigestion, ulcers and perforations. As sour taste has a fermentation action, it is toxic to the blood and can cause skin conditions like dermatitis, acne, eczema, edema, boils and psoriasis. The hot qualities may lead to acidic pH in the body and may cause burning in the throat, chest, heart, bladder and urethra.

Salty   Sea salt, rock salt and kelp are common examples of the salty taste. Water and Fire are the predominant elements. Salty is heating, heavy, oily and hydrophilous in nature. When used moderately, it relieves vata and intensifies kapha and pitta. Due to its Water element, it is laxative and, owing to the Fire element, it lessens spasm and pain of the colon. Like sweet and sour tastes, it is anabolic in action. When taken in moderation, it promotes growth and maintains water electrolyte balance. Salty taste is so strong that it nullifies the effect of all tastes. It stimulates salivation, improves the flavor of food, aids digestion, absorption and elimination of wastes.

Too much salt in the diet may cause aggravation of pitta and kapha. It makes the blood thick and viscous, causes hypertension and worsens skin conditions. Heating sensations, fainting, wrinkling and baldness may be due to excessive use of salt. Owing to its hydrophilous nature, it may induce edema or water retention. Patchy hair loss, ulcers, bleeding disorders, skin eruption, hyperacidity and hypertension may be disorders of overuse of the salty taste.

Pungent   The pungent taste is present in foods such as cayenne pepper, chili pepper, black pepper, onion, radish, garlic, mustard, ginger and asafoetida. Fire and Air are the important elements present in pungent. It is light, drying and heating in nature. It soothes kapha but excites pitta and vata. When used in the diet in moderation, it improves digestion, absorption and cleans the mouth. It clears the sinuses by stimulating nasal secretions and lacrimation. It aids circulation, breaks up clots, helps with the elimination of waste products and kills parasites and germs. It removes obstructions and brings clarity of perception.

Apart from these positive actions, pungent may cause negative reac tions when it is overused in the daily diet. It can kill sperm and ova, causing sexual debility in both sexes. It may induce burning, choking, fainting, fatigue with heat and thirst. If it leads to pitta aggravation, it can cause diarrhea, heartburn and nausea. With vata provocation from overuse of pungent taste, giddiness, tremors, insomnia and pain in the leg muscles may occur. Peptic ulcers, colitis and skin conditions may also result from excessive use.

Bitter   Examples of bitter taste are found in bitter melon, turmeric root, dandelion root, aloe vera, yellow dock, fenugreek, sandalwood, rhubarb and coffee. Bitter is the taste most lacking in the North American diet. It has the Air and Ether elements and is cool, light and dry in nature. It increases vata and decreases pitta and kapha. Though bitter is not delicious in itself, it promotes the flavor of the other tastes. It is anti-toxic and kills germs. It helps to relieve burning sensations, itching, fainting and obstinate skin disorders. It reduces fever and stimulates firmness of the skin and muscles. In a small dose, it can relieve intestinal gas and works as a digestive bitter tonic. It is drying to the system and causes a reduction in fat, bone marrow, urine and feces.

Over-consumption of the bitter taste may deplete plasma, blood, muscles, fat, bone marrow and semen, which may result in sexual debility. Extreme dryness and roughness, emaciation and weariness may be the result of excessive eating of the bitter taste. At times, it may induce dizziness and unconsciousness.

Astringent   Unripe banana, pomegranate, chickpeas, green beans, yellow split peas, okra, goldenseal, turmeric, lotus seed, alfalfa sprouts, mango seed, arjuna and alum are examples of astringent taste. It produces a typical drying, choking sensation in the throat. It is derived from the Air and Earth elements and is cooling, drying and heavy in nature. When taken in moderation, it calms pitta and kapha but excites vata. The astringent taste absorbs water and causes dryness of mouth, difficulty of speech and constipation. It aids in healing ulcers and stops bleeding by promoting clotting.

Excessive use of astringent foods may cause choking, absolute constipation, distention, obstruction of voice, heart spasm and stagnation of circulation. It may affect the sex drive leading to depletion of sperm. It can give rise to emaciation, convulsions, Bell's palsy, stroke paralysis and other neuromuscular vata disorders.

HOW THE TASTES AFFECT THE *DOSHAS*

Taste	Vata	Pitta	Kapha
Sweet	↓	↓	↑
Sour	↓	↑	↑
Salty	↓	↑	↑
Pungent	↑	↑	↓
Bitter	↑	↓	↓
Astringent	↑	↓	↓

↑ = increases and may lead to aggravation, ↓ = decreases and calms

According to Ayurveda, each taste used collectively or individually in the appropriate dose brings about balance of all the bodily systems and yields happiness and good health to all living beings. But if used improperly, much harm can result. So one should learn the normal and abnormal effects of these six tastes and make use of them properly in daily cooking.

Virya, Heating or Cooling Energy

When any medicinal herb or food substance is put in the mouth, the first experience is its taste. Later, or in some cases immediately, you feel its heating or cooling energy, either in the mouth or stomach. This change is all due to its action or potent energy called virya.

By self-experience, one can form general rules about what a taste "feels like" in the body. For example, the sweet taste has a cooling energy, owing to its heaviness. This action provokes kapha and is pleasing to pitta and vata. There are occasional exceptions to this rule. Honey and molasses are sweet but have heating energy. This unexpected effect is called *prabhav.* In the same way, sour taste is usually heating except in the instance of limes, which are cooling.

Vipaka, The Post-Digestive Effect

The final post-digestive effect of taste on the body, mind and consciousness is called vipaka. Sweet and salty tastes have a sweet vipaka, sour taste has a sour vipaka, but the vipaka of pungent, bitter and astringent tastes are all pungent. If one knows the taste, energy and post-digestive effect of a food or medicinal herb, it is simple to understand its action on bodily systems. This knowledge is essential for both healing and cooking.

To sum up, the first subjective experience of a substance on the tongue is taste (rasa); a short time later, one feels heating or cooling energy (virya); finally the substance has an action on urine, feces and sweat (vipaka). For instance, when an individual eats hot chili pepper, he or she will immediately experience its pungent taste, heating energy and the next day observe a burning sensation in the feces and urine.

Prabhav, The Specific Unexplained Action

When two substances of similar taste, energy and post-digestive effect show entirely different actions, this is called prabhav. There is no explanation for why this action takes place. It is beyond the logic of the theories we have been learning. *Ghee* (clarified butter) in doses of two teaspoons with a cup of milk is laxative but in a smaller dose, like half a teaspoon, is constipating. Why? The answer is prabhav. All gemstones, crystals and mantras aid healing due to their prabhav.

Prabhav is the specific, dynamic, hidden action of the awareness present in the substance.

Agni, The Digestive Fire

The concept of digestion in Ayurvedic medicine is quite remarkable. It begins with the external preparation and cooking of food. The basic requirements for this are a fireplace, heat, fuel, air, fire, pots, water, food and an organizer. The same things are needed for internal cooking or digestion.

The fireplace represents the intestines, and the fire is the agni. The fuel is yesterday's digested food which kindles the agni. The cooking pot is the stomach. The water is the gastric mucosal secretion, while the grain symbolizes the ingested food. The person or organizer is the prana. The ventilating air is the *samana* (a subtype of vata) which keeps the fire going. The stomach (or the pot) holds the food on the fire. The water in the pot (kapha) helps the uniform distribution of fire to each grain. The big fire within the fireplace is the central fire or digestive fire. Yesterday's digested food gives energy to the wall of the intestines to discharge digestive enzymes. These enzymes are the fuel to feed the agni. But without the organizer (prana) nothing can happen. The drawing on the following page is a visual explanation of this.

Our food contains solar energy which can only be utilized by the body through digestion. The external food substance has to be transformed into substances that can be absorbed and nourish the tissues. Many different enzymes are responsible for this transformation in the body. Ayurveda uses the term agni to describe these enzymes and metabolic processes. Without agni, it would be impossible to digest any of our food or any sensory data.

THE RELATIONSHIP BETWEEN INTERNAL AND EXTERNAL FIRE OR AGNI

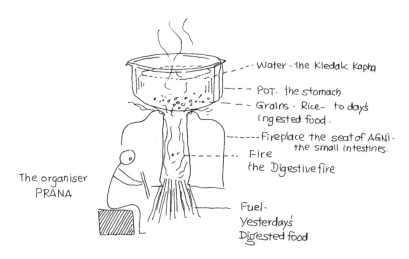

Water - the Kledak kapha

Pot. the stomach

Grains - Rice - to day's
ingested food.

Fireplace the seat of AGNI -
the small intestines.
Fire
the Digestive fire

The organiser
PRANA

Fuel -
Yesterday's
Digested food

In its normal, balanced state, agni sustains one's lifesaving, vitality and good health. It provides vital essence (ojas), preserves the life-breath (prana) and produces the luster of good health in the body. An individual endowed with adequate agni lives long and has excellent health. When agni is not functioning properly, the person begins to feel unwell. When this vital fire is extinguished, death soon follows.

The central agni is in the stomach. With five separate agnis in the liver and one for each of the seven tissue systems, there are a total of thirteen agnis governing the entire process of digestion and metabolism in an individual.

Many factors, such as detrimental lifestyle, diet, bad food combining and repressed emotions, can cause the bodily doshas to become aggravated. This soon disturbs agni, with the result that ingested food cannot be properly digested. The undigested food turns into a morbid, toxic, sticky substance, called *ama*.

Ama is the root cause of many diseases. The presence of ama in the systems leads to fatigue and a feeling of heaviness. It may induce constipation, indigestion, gases and diarrhea. At times, it can generate bad breath, perverted taste and mental confusion. The tongue acquires a thick coating (check your mirror!), and there may be generalized body ache and stiffness. Even food cravings often are due to the state of one's *agni*.

While considering Ayurvedic cooking, one should know in detail the concept of agni. Depending upon the nature of a person's agni, one can use specific condiments or seasonings and herbs and pickles, which may help to kindle agni and improve the quality of digestion. Depending on which dosha may be aggravated, agni can be balanced, irregular, too high or too low.

THE VARIETIES OF AGNI

Sama agni	balanced; tridoshic
Vishama agni	irregular; usually associated with vata
Tikshna agni	hyper; usually associated with pitta
Manda agni	hypo; usually associated with kapha

Sama Agni (Balanced metabolism)   When all the doshas are in balance according to the constitution, agni maintains its state of equilibrium and provides a balanced metabolism. Such a person digests any reasonable quantity and quality of food without adverse signs and symptoms. This is the state of perfect health. Neither food, season nor habit upsets these people with the gift of *sama agni*. They are blessed with good health and a long life. They have a calm, quiet, loving mind and great clarity of awareness and bliss. Stable health, surplus *ojas*, *tejas* and *prana*, and good immunity are the virtues of this agni condition.

Vishama Agni (Irregular metabolism)   As a result of aggravated vata, agni can undergo drastic changes. It becomes erratic and produces variable digestion, abdominal distention, constipation and colicky pain. At times, it may lead to diarrhea, a feeling of heaviness after food and gurgling of the intestines. The individual may get dry skin, cracking joints, sciatica, low backache, insomnia or deep-seated fear and anxiety. The subject may get cravings for fried food. The cold quality of vata slows down agni, and the mobile quality makes it fluctuate, resulting in irregular metabolism. Eventually, ama is produced and can be seen on the tongue as a brownish-black coating. Dry mouth, receding gums, muscle spasm and various other vata disorders may take place during the *vishama agni* state.

Tikshna Agni (Hypermetabolism)   Due to the hot, sharp and penetrating attributes of pitta, agni can become intense when pitta dosha is
increased. This causes hypermetabolism. In this condition the person has a
frequent desire to eat large quantities of food. After digestion, one gets dry
throat, lips, palate and heartburn. Hot flashes and hypoglycemia may be
seen, too. The liquid, sour and hot qualities of pitta may produce hyperacidity, gastritis, colitis and dysentery. Pain in the liver, nausea, vomiting and
other similar inflammatory conditions may occur. In some individuals, *tikshna agni* may lead to anger, hate and envy. The person becomes judgmental or critical toward everyone and everything. The subject can have
intense cravings for candy, cookies and chocolate. According to Ayurveda,
many *pitta* disorders have their origin in tikshna *agni*.

Manda Agni (Hypometabolism)   The water and earth molecules of
kapha dosha are heavy, slow and cool, which inhibit the light, sharp and
hot qualities of agni. As a result, agni may become dull and slow, leading to
slow metabolism. The individual with this type of agni cannot digest even a
normal diet properly. Even without eating, there is heaviness in the stomach, cold, congestion and cough. Over-salivation, loss of appetite, nausea
and mucoid vomiting can be seen. Others may show edema, obesity,
hypertension and diabetes. There will be lethargy, excessive sleep and cold
clammy skin. He or she will experience generalized weakness of the body.
Mentally there can be attachment, greed and possessiveness. The subject
may have a strong craving for hot, sharp, dry and spicy food. Almost all
kapha ailments are rooted in *manda agni*.

The Process of Digestion

It is beneficial to try to understand the digestive process, which initially
begins in the mouth when we chew our food. Mastication makes the food
soft, liquid, warm and easy to swallow. Saliva *(bodhaka kapha)* plays an
important role here. The food then passes into the stomach. For the next 90
minutes, mucous secretions from *kledaka kapha* liquefy it and break it
down into smaller pieces. The food becomes sweet during this stage. One
feels contented and full. This is the stage of digestion, via kledaka kapha,
where the sweet taste enters the plasma and raises the blood sugar.

During the subsequent 90 minutes, the food becomes sour in the stomach due to the secretion of hydrochloric acid, *pachaka pitta*. The mucous secretions mentioned above protect the walls of the stomach from the burning of pitta. The sour taste has Fire and Earth elements. The Fire element of pitta aids in digestion. It makes the stomach a little lighter. The foodstuff becomes softer and even more liquid, which enables the digestion and absorption through the stomach wall of certain light molecules of food material. The sour taste now enters into the plasma.

At the end of three hours, the pyloric valve is opened by samana, a subtype of vata, and the stomach empties into the duodenum, the first part of the small intestines. The bile from the liver and gallbladder, another form of pitta, mixes with the food and makes it salty, owing to the bile salts. The food which was sour and acidic in the stomach, when mixed with alkaline bile, becomes neutral and receives a salty taste, as acid and alkali together make salt and water. The food material becomes a watery, salty liquid. The Water and Fire elements of the salty taste help absorption. Now the salty taste will enter into the plasma. This salty taste continues until the food passes into the jejunum, the middle part of the small intestine.

In the second part of the jejunum, another "fire" of pitta from the small intestines makes the food pungent. The Fire and Air elements of the pungent taste improve digestion and assimilation in the jejunum. The food remains in the small intestines for about two and a half hours. At this point, the pungent taste enters the blood and plasma, promoting heat.

After the digestion in the small intestines, the food material passes into the cecum, the beginning of the large intestine, where it receives a bitter quality. The Air and space elements of this taste help the churning of the food material. The absorption of minerals is also governed by these elements. The bitter taste now enters into the plasma.

Lastly, the food enters the ascending colon. At this stage the astringent taste becomes predominant and makes the food material solid, owing to the Earth and Air elements. The astringent taste entering into the plasma makes the person feel light. A combination of vata and pitta discriminate essential and nonessential food material. The bitter and astringent tastes help to improve the absorption and stimulate the movement of the colon via *apana,* a subtype of vata. When the solid wastes pass into the rectum, vata stimulates mass peristalsis (muscle contractions) to evacuate the bowels.

The entire digestive process requires about six to eight hours, and the food has gone through different stages according to the changes in various tastes. However, digestion does not end with the absorption by the colon. Very subtle digestion now occurs in that the nourishment must arrive at and be used by the cells of our plasma, blood, bones, fat, muscle, nerves and reproductive system. With the help of yet another pitta "fire" or agni, this digested food is further altered at the cellular level into the pure energy of consciousness and nourishes the mind.

Gourds

Chapter 4

FOOD COMBINING

It is no surprise to see on the market today so many digestive and dietary aids for the stomach, along with pills for gas and indigestion. Most of these conditions likely begin with poor food combining. This is a subject of much debate amid the growing concern about diet and the many theories on the topic.

Ayurveda, an ancient holistic science of healing, offers a logical approach for determining correct diet based upon the elements comprising an individual's constitution: vata, pitta and kapha. This approach is quite different from the contemporary view of a balanced diet, based on eating from various food groups. Ayurveda believes that understanding the individual is the key to finding a truly balanced diet. It teaches that the gastric fire or agni in the stomach and digestive tract is the main gate through which nutrients enter the tissues and then pass along to individual cells, to maintain the life functions. Proper digestion is closely connected to the strength of agni (gastric fire). The nutritionist should give consideration to the four types of agni (See "The Varieties of Agni" on page 41.) when making suggestions concerning diet.

According to Ayurveda, every food has its own taste (rasa), a heating or cooling energy (virya) and a post-digestive effect (vipaka). Some also possess prabhav, an unexplained effect. So while it is true that an individual's agni largely determines how well or poorly food is digested, food combinations are also of great importance. When two or more foods having different taste, energy and post-digestive effect are combined, agni can become overloaded, inhibiting the enzyme system and resulting in the production of toxins. Yet these same foods, if eaten separately, might well stimulate agni, be digested more quickly and even help to burn ama.

Poor combining can produce indigestion, fermentation, putrefaction and gas formation and, if prolonged, can lead to toxemia and disease. For example, eating bananas with milk can diminish agni, change the intestinal flora, produce toxins and may cause sinus congestion, cold, cough and allergies. Although both of these foods have a sweet taste and a cooling energy, their post-digestive effect is very different—bananas are sour while milk is sweet. This causes confusion to our digestive system and may result in toxins, allergies and other imbalances.

Similarly, milk and melons should not be eaten together. Both are cooling, but milk is laxative and melon diuretic. Milk requires more time for digestion. Moreover the stomach acid required to digest the melon causes the milk to curdle, so Ayurveda advises against taking milk with sour foods.

These incompatible food combinations not only disturb the digestion but also cause confusion in the intelligence of our cells, which can lead to many different diseases.

Before you say "This is MUCH too complicated, how will I ever figure it out?", there are some useful guidelines to introduce you to these concepts. And remember that Ayurveda is a strong proponent of the "go slowly" school of thought.

You might want to introduce yourself to food combining by *eating fruit by itself*, as many fruits create a sour and indigestible "wine" in the stomach when mixed with other food. Once you have adopted this change into your eating habits, try other suggestions from the list below. As a general principal, avoid eating lots of raw and cooked foods together or fresh foods with leftovers.

There are various factors that can help lessen the possible effect of a bad food combination.

• A strong digestive fire (if we are so blessed) can be the most powerful tool of all to deal with "bad" food combinations.

• Different quantities of each food involved in a combination can sometimes help significantly. For instance equal quantities *by weight* of ghee and honey are a bad combination—ghee is cooling, but honey is heating—whereas mixing a 2 to 1 ratio is not toxic. The reason? Prabhav, the unexplainable.

• Very often spices and herbs are added in Ayurvedic cooking to help make foods compatible or to ease a powerful effect, e.g., cooling cilantro in very spicy food.

Continued on page 48

INCOMPATIBLE FOOD COMBINING[A]

Don't eat:	*With:*
Beans	fruit, cheese, eggs, fish, milk, meat, yogurt
Eggs	fruit, especially melons; beans, cheese, fish, kitchari, MILK[b], meat, yogurt
Fruit	As a rule, with *any other food*. (There are exceptions, such as certain cooked combinations, as well as dates and milk, which have the same rasa, virya and vipaka.)
Grains	fruit; tapioca
Honey[c]	when mixed with an equal amount of *ghee* by weight (i.e., 1 tsp. honey with 3 tsp. ghee); boiled or cooked honey.
Hot drinks	mangos, cheese, fish, meat, starch, yogurt
Lemon	cucumbers, milk, tomatoes, yogurt
Melons	EVERYTHING – especially dairy, eggs, fried food, grains, starches. Melons more than most fruit should be eaten alone or left alone.
Milk	BANANAS, cherries, melons, sour fruits; bread containing yeast, fish, kitchari, meat, yogurt
Nightshades (potato, tomato, eggplant)	melon, cucumber, dairy products
Radishes	bananas, raisins, milk
Tapioca	fruit, especially banana and mango; beans, raisins, jaggery
Yogurt	fruit, cheese, eggs, fish, hot drinks, meat, MILK, nightshades

a. These guidelines are by no means an exhaustive list. It must be remembered that a proper Ayurvedic diet should consider nutritional value, constitution, seasons, age and any disease condition.
b. Foods in CAPITALS are the most difficult combinations.
c. According to ancient Ayurvedic literature, honey should never be cooked. If cooked, the molecules become a non-homogenized glue that adheres to mucous membranes and clogs subtle channels, producing toxins. Uncooked honey is nectar. Cooked honey is considered poison.

Continued from page 46

• If our bodies have become accustomed to a certain food combination through many years of use, such as eating cheese with apples, then it is likely that our body has made some adaptation or become accustomed to this. Which is not to say that we should continue this practice, but to explain why the newcomer to apples and cheese may experience a strong case of indigestion whilst the "old-timer" digests it adequately.

• Antidotes, like cardamom in coffee, or ghee and black pepper with potatoes, often can help alleviate some of the negative effects. (Coffee is stimulating and ultimately depressing to the system, and potatoes cause gas).

• If foods with different and possibly aggravating qualities, such as a mixture of vegetables, are cooked together in the same pot, the foods tend to learn how to get along. Using appropriate spices and herbs helps with this too.

• Eating a "bad" combination occasionally usually does not upset the digestion too much.

Some Useful Tips To Aid Digestion:

Eat ½ teaspoon fresh grated ginger with a pinch of rock salt before each meal to stimulate agni.

Salt also aids digestion, and helps to retain water.

Alkalis help digestion and regulate gastric fire.

Ghee stimulates agni and improves digestion.

Small sips of warm water during a meal will aid digestion and absorption of food. Do not drink iced water as it slows agni and digestion. Indeed ice water should not be taken under most circumstances, as it is too shocking to the system.

Proper chewing is essential to good digestion, ensuring food gets thoroughly mixed with saliva.

A cup of *lassi* at the end of a meal also aids the digestive process. Make by blending ¼ cup yogurt with 2 pinches of ginger and cumin powder in 1 cup water.

Ideally, one should fill the stomach with one-third food, one-third liquid and one-third should be empty.

Chapter 5

SETTING UP AN AYURVEDIC KITCHEN AND PANTRY

Before you begin to cook the Ayurvedic recipes in this book, you will want to have some basic foods, spices and utensils on hand for this way of cooking. Use the list that follows as a guideline to slowly build an Ayurvedic kitchen. Just one of the benefits of this kitchen is that many of the basic ingredients are dried and happy resting on your kitchen shelves, so that when you have six unexpected guests for supper you can always prepare an Ayurvedic meal.

Every act you perform around food should be in a loving, honoring and sacred manner. Whether you are growing the food, selecting it in a supermarket or preparing it for cooking, the amount of loving awareness and respect you give it transfers exactly to the food and to the hungry stomachs. Food that is prepared in a loving manner can bring truly healing results to everyone.

Utensils for your Ayurvedic kitchen

One (at least) heavy cast-iron frying pan
One chapati skillet, if possible (saucer-shaped, without steep sides)
Two or three medium-sized pots with lids—stainless steel is best
One soup pot with lid—also stainless steel
One small metal pot for melting ghee
One deep pot for frying—cast iron is best
One heavy frying pan with lid
Two or three mixing bowls, measuring cup and spoons
Hand eggbeater
Large metal spoon and soup ladle
Blender
Chapati, or other rolling pin, and cutting board

Basic spices you will need:
(quantity is only a guideline!)
[Spices marked with » are in the
  Herbs for Healing section]
»Ajwan - 1 oz.
»Bay leaves - 1 oz.
»Black mustard seeds - 4 oz.
Black cumin seeds - 1 oz.
»Black pepper, ground - 2 oz.
»Black pepper, whole - 1 oz.
»Brown cumin seeds, whole - 4 oz.
»Brown cumin seeds, ground - 2 oz.
»Cardamom, whole - 1 oz.
»Cardamom, ground - 1 oz.
Cayenne - 1 oz.
»Cinnamon bark - 2 oz.
»Cinnamon powder - 2 oz.
»Coriander seeds - 4 oz.
Curry leaves - 1 pkg., fresh or dried
Dill seed - 1 oz.
»Fennel seeds - 4 oz.
Fenugreek seeds - 1 oz.
»Ginger, dry - 2 oz.
Hing (Asafoetida) - 1 can (should be the
  compound, rather than pure)
Masala powder - 2 oz.
»Nutmeg, ground or whole - 1 oz.
»Saffron - 1 small box (1 g.)
»Salt - 4 oz.
»Turmeric - 6-8 oz.
Whole cloves - 1 oz.

Nuts and seeds:
Charoli (Indian grocery) - 4 oz.
Almonds, whole-4 oz.; sliced - 2 oz.
Peanuts, raw & whole - 4 oz.
Sesame seeds, brown - 4 oz.
Poppy seeds, brown or white - 2 oz.
Coconut, shredded - ½ lb.

Oils:
Ghee - at least 1 lb.
Sunflower, safflower, canola or other,
  depending on constitution

Rice and beans:
Basmati rice, white - 5 lb.
Poha (rice flakes) - 1 lb.
Split yellow mung dal - 2 lb.
Whole mung beans - 1 lb.
Tur dal - 1 lb.
Urad dal - 1 lb.
Red lentils - 1 lb.
Dried green peas - 1 lb.
Kidney beans - 1 lb.
Pinto beans - 1 lb.
Black-eyed peas - 1 lb.
Chickpeas (garbanzos) - 1 lb.

Grains, flours, etc.:
Cream of Wheat™ - I lb.
Cream of Rice™ - ½ lb.
Flour, all-purpose - 1 lb.
Flour, whole wheat - 2 lb.
Tapioca - 1 lb.
Indian vermicelli, toasted - 1 pkg
Cornmeal - 1 lb.
Garbanzo flour - 1 lb.
Baking soda - 2 oz.

Sweets:
Sucanat, turbinado or
  jaggery sugar - 1 lb.
Raw honey - ½ lb.
Any others to suit your constitution

Dried fruit:
Dates - 1 lb.
Kokam fruits - 1 package

Fresh things:
A variety of fresh vegetables
Cilantro
Green chilies
Onions
Limes
Fresh ginger root - 3-4 oz.
Fresh garlic bulb - 1
Milk, yogurt, buttermilk

Chapter 6

MENU PLANNING

Winter and Summer Meals for Vata, Pitta and Kapha

Because many of those using this cookbook may be new to Ayurveda, we thought it would be helpful to provide sample menu planning and guidelines using a few of the recipes.*

Once you become familiar with the book, you will begin to develop menus for your own constitution, tastes and lifestyle. When planning a meal, it is important to pay attention to the six tastes—sweet, sour, salty, pungent, bitter and astringent—as well as to the food groups.** Ideally, at your noon and evening meals, you will plan your meals so that all 6 tastes will be present in the food. The front cover of this book and its explanatory drawing show a meal with all the tastes. For example, in the lunch and supper menus that follow, fresh lime or lemon is recommended frequently. This can be squeezed over the kitchari, vegetables or other main dish and provides the sour taste necessary for the meal.

As you begin to make up your own menus, it is useful to review the Food Combining section and keep these principles in mind, especially the one about eating fruit by itself and waiting for at least an hour to eat any other food or drink.

NOTES:

*In the menus, recipes that appear in this book are designated with capital letters, i.e., Saffron Rice.

**These menus have been designed to correspond to the current food group categories set by the U.S. Department of Agriculture.

VATA MEALS FOR WINTER

Breakfast	Lunch
Upma or Creamed Wheat Porridge (G)* milk for porridge, if desired (D) Chai or Breakfast Tea, with sweetener, if desired (O)	Chapati or Spicy Puri "Plain Rice" (with soup) (G) Carrot Subji (V) Mung Dal Kitchari (Vata) or Tur Dal Soup No. 2 (M) Almond or Rice Khir or Sweet Lassi (D) Fresh lemon (squeeze on subji) (O) Sesame Chutney (O) Vata Tea (O)

Snack	Dinner
ginger snaps or sesame snaps (G) seasonal, sweet fruit (V) hot spiced milk, especially good before bed (don't have this if you've eaten an egg) (D) herbal teas or grain coffee with milk (O)	Chapati or whole wheat tortilla (G) baked sweet potato with ghee (V) one egg or roasted, ground sunflower seeds (over potato) (M) fresh lemon (O) Creamed Wheat Squares (O) Dinner Tea (O)

*(G) = Grains, breads, cereals, rice and pasta
 (V) = Vegetables and fruits
 (M) = Meat and meat alternatives
 (D) = Dairy, milk and milk products
 (O) = Other foods, condiments, sweets and beverages

Vata Meals for Summer

Breakfast	Lunch
oatmeal muffins or pancakes with ghee (G) seasonal sweet fruit (eaten 1 hour before any other food) (V) Chai or Breakfast Tea with sweetener, if desired (O)	Chapati (G) Saffron Rice (with the subji) (G) Mixed Vegetable Subji (V) or Mung Dal Kitchari (Vata) with ghee and cilantro (M) Sweet Lassi or tea (D) fresh lemon or lime (O) Peanut Chutney (O) Lunch Tea or Lassi (O) (have tea 1 hour after Lassi)

Snack	Dinner
oatmeal cookies (G) seasonal fruit (V) soaked, peeled almonds (M) hot spiced milk, before bed (optional) (D) herbal teas such as chamomile or cumin (O)	Spinach or Okra Subji (V) Tapioca Kitchari (M) (Grains should not be eaten with Tapioca Kitchari) (G) fresh lemon or lime for Kitchari (O) Sweet Potato Khir (O) Dinner Tea (O)

*(G) = Grains, breads, cereals, rice and pasta
(V) = Vegetables and fruits
(M) = Meat and meat alternatives
(D) = Dairy, milk and milk products
(O) = Other foods, condiments, sweets and beverages

PITTA MEALS FOR WINTER

Breakfast	*Lunch*
Creamed Wheat Porridge or oatmeal (G) milk or *ghee* with porridge, if desired (D) Chai or Breakfast Tea with maple syrup or sweetener, if desired (O)	Chapati (G) "Plain Rice" or Saffron Rice (with bhaji) (G) Squash Subji (V) Mung Dal Kitchari (Pitta) or Kidney Bean Bhaji (M) Carrot Halva and/or Pachak Lassi or tea (D) squeeze of lime (O) Cilantro Chutney (O) Lunch Tea or Lassi (have tea 1 hour after Lassi) (O)
Snacks	*Dinner*
oatmeal cookies (G) sweet apple or pear (V) hot almond milk or spiced milk with ghee and turmeric—best ½ hr. before bed (D)	Chapati or Puri (G) Potato Subji No. 1 (V) Lentil Soup or egg white omelet (M) squeeze of lime (O) Agni Tea (O)

*(G) = Grains, breads, cereals, rice and pasta
 (V) = Vegetables and fruits
 (M) = Meat and meat alternatives
 (D) = Dairy, milk and milk products
 (O) = Other foods, condiments, sweets and beverages

PITTA MEALS FOR SUMMER

Breakfast	Lunch
oat bran muffin with *ghee* or oat or wheat granola (G) seasonal fruit (V) (eaten 1 hour before any other food) milk for cereal, if desired (D) Mint Chai or Agni Tea (O)	Chapati (G) basmati or "Plain Rice" (G) Bitter Melon or Green Bean Subji, small salad with oil (V) Pachak Lassi (D) fresh lime for beans (O) Mint Chutney (O) Lunch Tea (have tea 1 hour after Lassi) (O)
Snacks	Dinner
coconut cookies (G) seasonal fresh fruit (V) natural ice cream or cool milk with rosewater (D) Mint Chai or mint tea (O)	Chapati (G) Fried Rice (G) Mixed Vegetable Soup (V) roasted, ground sunflower seeds to sprinkle on soup (M) fresh lime for soup (O) Dinner Tea (O)

*(G) = Grains, breads, cereals, rice and pasta
(V) = Vegetables and fruits
(M) = Meat and meat alternatives
(D) = Dairy, milk and milk products
(O) = Other foods, condiments, sweets and beverages

Kapha Meals for Winter

Breakfast	Lunch
creamed rye or spiced oatmeal porridge (G) or suitable fruit (V) Breakfast Tea, with honey (1 tsp.), if desired (O)	corn tortilla or cornbread (G) Cabbage Subji (with Kitchari only) (V) Mung Dal Kitchari (Kapha) or tofu and vegetables (M) fresh lime (O) Green Mango Chutney (O) Kapha Tea (O)

Snacks	Dinner
popcorn (no salt or butter) or unsalted corn chips with salsa (G) apples or pears or other suitable fruit (V) 1 cup suitable herbal tea (O)	un-yeasted rye bread or rye crackers, Poha with Potatoes (G) Corn Soup (V) (protein from corn and rye combination) (M) fresh lime (O) Cilantro Chutney (O) Tea Masala (O)

*(G) = Grains, breads, cereals, rice and pasta
 (V) = Vegetables and fruits
 (M) = Meat and meat alternatives
 (D) = Dairy, milk and milk products
 (O) = Other foods, condiments, sweets and beverages

KAPHA MEALS FOR SUMMER

Breakfast	Lunch
puffed millet or oat granola (G) ½ cup skim goat milk or soy milk, if desired (D) Kapha Tea with 1 tsp. honey, if desired (O)	un-yeasted rye bread or spiced cooked millet or barley (G) Green Bean Subji (V) (protein is from bean and grain combination) (M) fresh lime or lemon (O) Carrot Chutney (O) Lunch Tea (O)
Snacks	Dinner
1 or 2 rice cakes (G) suitable fruit or juice in season (V) dry roasted, unsalted sunflower seeds (M) 1 cup herbal tea such as ginger, cinnamon or mint (O)	mixed green salad with lemon or lime juice (V) Tapioca Kitchari (M) (Grains should not be eaten with Tapioca Kitchari) (G) fresh lime or lemon (O) Turmeric Chutney (O) Agni Tea (O)

*(G) = Grains, breads, cereals, rice and pasta
(V) = Vegetables and fruits
(M) = Meat and meat alternatives
(D) = Dairy, milk and milk products
(O) = Other foods, condiments, sweets and beverages

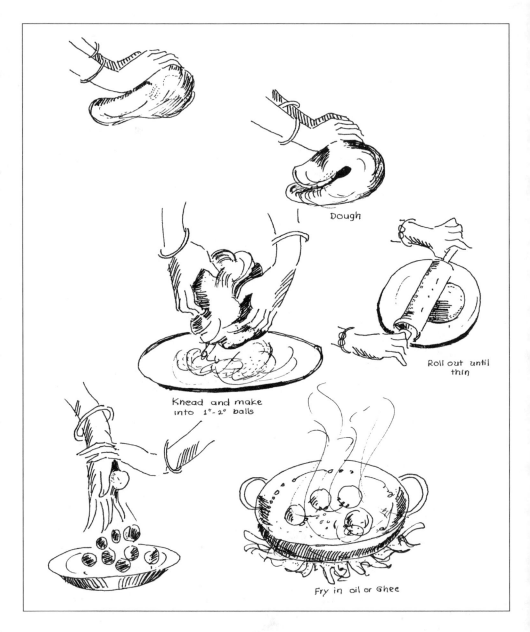

Dough

Knead and make
into 1"- 2" balls

Roll out until
thin

Fry in oil or Ghee

PURI PREPARATION
(Plain Puri Recipe - page 153)

Chapter 7

RECIPES

Helpful Hints about Ayurvedic Cooking

Ayurvedic cuisine may be unique in the world for its emphasis on making sure each dish is cooked and spiced in a way to achieve maximum digestibility, as well as superb taste and food value. Ayurveda does not have a precise line between herbs and spices used for enhancing taste and digestibility and those used in healing. So while they add flavor to our foods, they are also adding healing benefits as well. And, as mentioned in the section on *Setting Up Your Ayurvedic Kitchen*, the most important ingredient in cooking any of these recipes is the love and respect you bring to the food you will prepare and serve.

Every spice and herb in these recipes is included for several important reasons: to enhance the taste, to stimulate the digestive fire, to increase digestibility and absorption, and to help counteract any incompatible food combinations (see the section on *Food Combining*). The quantities of spices and herbs suggested in each recipe are to provide both an introduction and a guideline for you. The seasoning has been made intentionally mild the better to suit all constitutions. Once you become familiar with the recipes, you may want to vary the spicing for your own tastes; simply try to keep the proportions in balance. *If you have been fortunate enough to sample some of Usha Lad's cooking, you would find that she uses at least double the quantities of seasonings suggested here.* Like most good cooks, Usha Lad cooks by feel rather than precise measurement, and she may vary the spicing according to the season, the diners or other variables.

When you are ready to begin cooking, you will notice that many of the recipes begin in a similar way. Ghee or oil is heated over a medium heat in a heavy saucepan, then black mustard seeds and cumin seeds are sautéed in the oil for a few moments until they pop. This "popping" liberates the

prana or vital energy of the seeds, increasing the food value. Next hing—
the compounded kind not the pure stuff—is often added. This helps dispel
gas caused by the beans and some food combinations. Next other seeds
and herbs are added, along with onions, ginger, curry leaves, etc. Ground
spices are added last because of their tendency to burn. Then the rice or
vegetable is put in and stirred to coat it well with the spices. Your kitchen
will be full of the pungent aromas from the sautéing. As you become familiar with the seasonings and the Ayurvedic cooking techniques, you may
also want to adapt them to your own favorite recipes.

In recipes that use fresh ginger, it is specified to peel and chop it finely.
If the ginger is very fresh and its skin is thin and smooth, you may simply
wash it well and grate it, skin and all.

Unusual foods or processes are discussed within the recipe Particular
cautions for specific doshas are listed after each recipe, as are any special
healing values of a recipe. There is also a glossary of unfamiliar foods and
terms at the back of the book.

The Editor

Soups

In Ayurvedic cooking, soups are most often eaten with the main course. Soups made of beans, peas or lentils and spices are the most common, and provide the complement to a grain (usually rice) to make a very digestible, high protein dish.

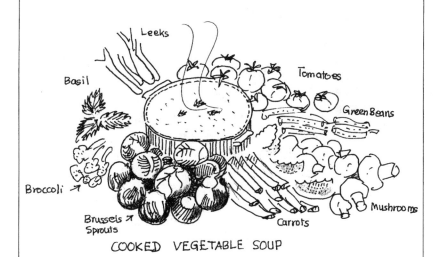

COOKED VEGETABLE SOUP

Kokam Soup

Serves 4

9	dried Kokam fruits
4	cups water
2	tablespoons ghee
1	teaspoon cumin seeds
4	curry leaves, fresh or dried
1	tablespoon fresh cilantro leaves, chopped
2	bay leaves
2	tablespoons chickpea flour
¼	teaspoon cinnamon
2	pinches cayenne or black pepper
¼	teaspoon ground cloves
¾	teaspoon salt
1	tablespoon jaggery (or Sucanat) sugar

Wash and soak the Kokam fruits in l cup of the water for 10-20 minutes. Then squeeze the fruit several times into this water and remove it from the water. Heat a saucepan until medium-hot and add the ghee, cumin seeds, curry leaves, cilantro and bay leaves. Stir or shake the pan until the seeds pop. Pour in the fruit water plus 2 more cups of the water.

Mix the chickpea flour with the last cup of water very well, then add to the soup. Stir to prevent lumps forming. Add the cinnamon, cayenne, clove, salt and jaggery. Stir and boil gently for 5 minutes.

Do not store this in a metal container (except for a stainless steel one), for the acid in the fruit will react to the metal and turn the soup bad.

Kokam is available from Indian grocery stores. It is sour and heating. This soup is a good appetizer and digestive. It stimulates normal gastric fire and detoxifies the body of toxins (ama). It is also an excellent blood cleanser. If taken before the meal, it acts as an appetizer. At the end of the meal, it is a digestive. Do not use for breakfast!

Okay for pitta and kapha if not more than one cup is taken.

Medicinal uses: Good for diarrhea, heart, swellings, hemorrhoids and worms. It can help as an anti-allergic agent in skin rash.

Corn Soup

Serves 4

5   cobs of fresh corn
5   cups water
1   inch piece of fresh ginger, peeled and chopped fine
1   heaping tablespoon cilantro leaves, chopped
¼   cup water
2   tablespoons ghee
1   teaspoon cumin seeds
½   teaspoon garam masala
¼   teaspoon black pepper
1   pinch salt

Cut the corn off the washed cobs to make about 4 cups. Put the corn in a blender with 2 cups of the water and blend until creamy. Pour into a bowl and set aside.

Now put the ginger, cilantro and ¼ cup water into the blender and liquefy for 1 minute.

Heat a soup pot on medium heat and add the ghee and cumin seeds. When the seeds pop, stir in the garam masala. Then add the blended spices, blended corn and the black pepper.

Add the rest of the water and mix well.

Boil gently until tender, about 15 - 20 minutes, uncovered. Stir occasionally.

Add salt just before serving.

Garnish with cilantro leaves and black pepper to taste.

Corn soup is a good breakfast food.

Corn Soup balances tridosha, but its long term effect is drying for vata. So vata can eat occasionally and pitta in moderation. The cilantro helps remove some of the heat for pitta.

Medicinal uses: This is a good food for people with high cholesterol or who are suffering from obesity as long as they cook it without the ghee.

Green Mung Soup

Serves 4 to 6

1   cup whole green mung beans
5-6 cups water
2   tablespoons safflower oil
1   teaspoon cumin seeds
1   teaspoon black mustard seeds
1   pinch hing
2   large cloves garlic, chopped
5   curry leaves, fresh or dried
1   small handful cilantro leaves, chopped
½   teaspoon turmeric
½   teaspoon masala powder
½   teaspoon salt

Wash the beans twice and soak overnight in plenty of water. Drain.
Add the beans and 4 cups of the water to a soup pot and bring to a boil. Stir beans occasionally to prevent sticking. Cook on medium heat, uncovered, for 30 minutes.
Add 1 more cup of the water and continue to cook for another 15-20 minutes or until beans are tender. Set aside.
Heat the oil in a small pan or frying pan until medium hot, then add the mustard seeds, cumin seeds and hing. In a moment, when the seeds pop, stir in the garlic and brown lightly.
Add the curry leaves, cilantro, turmeric and masala powder. Mix quickly. Stir this spice mixture into the soup. Add the salt. Add some or all of the last cup of water, depending on how thick you want the soup.
Bring to a boil for 2 minutes and serve.

▨ Green mung is sweet and astringent with a cooling energy. This soup is a high protein combination and an energizer when used with rice and chapatis. It is light to digest and balances the three *doshas*. People with indigestion can easily digest Green Mung Soup. One or two cups are good with the main meal. The hing helps to remove the gas-creating effect of the beans.

Medicinal Uses: A good food for conditions of fever or eye problems.

Red Lentil Soup

Serves 4 to 6

1	cup red lentils
5	cups water
2	teaspoons safflower oil
1	teaspoon cumin seeds
1	teaspoon black mustard seeds
1	pinch hing
2	large cloves garlic, chopped
5	curry leaves, fresh or dried
1	small handful cilantro leaves, chopped
½	teaspoon turmeric
1	teaspoon masala powder
½	teaspoon salt

Wash the beans twice and soak overnight in plenty of water. Drain.

Add the beans and 4 cups of the water to a soup pot and bring to a boil. Cook on medium heat, uncovered, for 30 minutes. Stir beans occasionally to prevent sticking.

Add 1 more cup of the water and continue to cook for another 15-20 minutes or until beans are tender. Set aside.

Heat the oil in a small pan or frying pan until medium hot, then add the mustard seeds, cumin seeds and hing. In a moment, when the seeds pop, stir in the garlic and brown lightly.

Add the curry leaves, cilantro, turmeric and masala powder. Mix quickly.

Stir this spice mixture into the soup, then add the salt. Add some or all of the last cup of water, depending on the how thick you want the soup.

Bring to a boil for 2 minutes and serve with rice and chapati or bread.

⊞ Although this soup is *tridoshic*, the light and dry quality may stimulate *vata*, so *vata* should not eat it more than twice a week. The spice in this recipe make the lentils okay for *pitta*.

Sautéing the garlic helps to get rid of its gas-producing qualities.

Masala powder can be bought at most spice stores or make your own with the recipe in this book.

Medicinal Uses: A good food to take during flu and diarrhea. Red lentils are a good source of iron, so are a good blood builder and liver cleanser.

Mixed Vegetable Soup

V↓ P↓ K↓

Serves 4

4   cups mixed vegetables (carrots, green beans, squash, etc.)
8   cups water
1   teaspoon cumin seeds
6   whole peppercorns
1   inch piece of cinnamon stick
10 cloves
10 cardamom pods
2   tablespoons ghee
½   teaspoon salt

Wash and cut the vegetables into bite-sized pieces.
Put the vegetables and water in a large soup pot, cover and cook on medium heat until just tender. Set aside in a bowl.
Meanwhile grind to a fine powder the cumin seeds, peppercorns, cinnamon stick, cardamom pods and cloves in a mortar and pestle or use a blender.
Heat a soup pot on medium heat and add the ghee, then the ground spices. Sauté a moment, being careful not to burn them.
Add the vegetables and 4 cups of the broth. Boil for 2 minutes.
Stir in the salt and serve.

▨ Each vegetable has a specific calming or stimulating effect on the *doshas* when eaten alone. For instance, carrots pacify vata and kapha but may aggravate pitta because of their heating quality. Cooking vegetables together and with these seasonings makes a soup that is tridoshic, good for all constitutions.

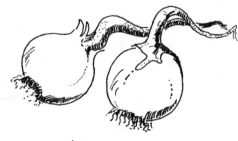

ONIONS

Spinach Soup

Serves 4

1   large bunch spinach (about 4 cups when chopped)
5   cups water
½   small green chili, chopped
1½ inch piece of fresh ginger, peeled and chopped fine
1   small handful fresh cilantro leaves
½   cup water
2   tablespoons ghee
1   teaspoon cumin seeds
1   teaspoon black mustard seeds
1   pinch hing
4   curry leaves, fresh or dried
½   teaspoon salt
     ground black pepper

Remove the stems of the spinach. Wash and chop the leaves.
Put the spinach in a blender with 4 cups of the water and blend for 2 minutes on medium speed. Remove from blender.
Add the ½ cup water, chili, ginger and cilantro to the blender and mix until liquefied.
Heat a soup pot on medium heat and add the ghee, cumin seeds, mustard seeds, hing and curry leaves. Cook a moment until the seeds pop.
Pour in the blended spices, blended spinach, salt and the last cup of water and stir well. Bring to a boil and boil gently, uncovered, for 10-15 minutes.
Add black pepper to taste when serving.

Cooked spinach is astringent, sour, and heating with a sweet vipaka. By itself, it is stimulating to pitta but pacifying to vata and kapha if used in moderation. It is heavy to digest and undigested spinach may cause gas and constipation. This spinach soup with its seasonings is a good digestive and can be used by all doshas occasionally, for its medicinal properties.
Pitta should use in moderation.

Medicinal Uses: The soup is good for asthma, as a blood builder and decongestant. Spinach is not so good for the patient with kidney stones and gallstones or for those with gouty arthritis and edema, as it causes water retention.

Tomato Soup

Serves 4

3   good-sized tomatoes
4   cups water
1   tablespoon unsweetened, shredded coconut
1½ inch piece of fresh ginger, peeled and chopped fine
1   clove garlic, peeled and chopped
½   small, green chili, chopped
1   small handful fresh cilantro leaves
½   cup water
2   tablespoons ghee
1   teaspoon black mustard seeds
1   teaspoon cumin seeds
4   curry leaves, fresh or dried
¼   teaspoon cinnamon
¾   teaspoon salt
½   cup water
1   tablespoon jaggery or other sweetener

Wash the whole tomatoes and put them in a soup pot with the 4 cups of water. Cover and cook until the tomatoes are tender and the skins pull off easily.
Let the tomatoes cool down a little. Remove and discard the skins. Pour the tomatoes and the cooking water into a blender and blend until smooth. Remove from blender.
Now add to the blender the coconut, ginger, garlic, chili and cilantro with the ½ cup water. Blend until liquefied.
Heat a soup pot on medium and add the ghee, cumin seeds, mustard seeds and curry leaves. Stir until the seeds pop, then add the blended coconut mixture.
Cook for a moment then pour in the blended tomatoes, cinnamon, salt, sugar and last ½ cup water. Bring to a boil, cover and turn off the heat.

◆ Due to its sour and heating quality, this may aggravate pitta, so it should not be eaten more than once or twice a week. Tomatoes by themselves disturb the tridoshic balance, but in this recipe are tridoshic. This soup is digestive, laxative and calms vata and pitta. Tomatoes are a member of the nightshade family. People with kidney stones, gallstones and gout should not eat tomatoes or other nightshades.

Tur Dal Soup No. 1

Serves 4 to 6

1   cup tur dal
9   cups water
½   teaspoon turmeric
2   pinches hing
1   tablespoon ghee
1   teaspoon black mustard seeds
1   teaspoon cumin seeds
½   teaspoon salt

Wash the tur dal 2 times.

Add the tur dal, 4 cups of the water, the turmeric and hing to a soup pot and cook uncovered over medium heat for 30 minutes. Stir occasionally to keep from sticking.

After the 30 minutes, add 4 more cups of water and continue cooking until tender, about 50-60 minutes more.

Add the last cup of water and beat well with an eggbeater.

Heat a small saucepan and add the ghee, salt, mustard seeds, and cumin seeds. Sauté for a moment until the seeds pop. Add this to the soup and boil for 1 minute. Remove from the heat and serve.

Tur dal is astringent, sweet and heating. This soup will be calming for vata and kapha, and is especially beneficial when eaten with basmati rice as a main meal.

The pungent post-digestive effect of the dal may aggravate pitta, so occasional use (once or twice a week) is recommended.

Medicinal uses: Good for strengthening muscles and as a blood builder. Also great for skin, eyes, bones and joints.

Tur Dal Soup No. 2

Serves 4 to 6

1   cup tur dal
9   cups water
½   teaspoon turmeric
2   pinches of hing
2   tablespoons safflower oil
1   teaspoon black mustard seeds
1   teaspoon cumin seeds
5   curry leaves, fresh or dried
1   small handful cilantro leaves, chopped
2   pinches masala powder
1   teaspoon salt

Wash the tur dal twice.

Add the tur dal, 4 cups of the water, the turmeric and hing to a soup pot and cook uncovered over medium heat for 30 minutes. Stir occasionally to keep from sticking.

After the 30 minutes, add 4 more cups water and continue cooking until tender, about 50-60 minutes more.

Beat the soup with an eggbeater until smoothly mixed. Add the last cup of water.

Heat a small saucepan and add the oil, mustard seeds, cumin seeds, curry leaves, cilantro and masala. Sauté for a moment until the seeds pop. Add this to the soup.

Bring the soup to a boil for a minute or two, add the salt and serve.

▦ Pitta must use this in moderation, once or twice a week.

Properties are the same as for Plain Tur Dal Soup.

Varan Phala

Serves 8 with large portions

1½ cups tur dal
8   cups water
½   teaspoon turmeric
¼   cup sunflower oil
1   teaspoon mustard seeds
1   teaspoon cumin seeds
1   pinch hing
½   teaspoon turmeric
½   teaspoon salt
7   curry leaves, fresh or dried
1   small green chili, chopped <u>or</u> ½ teaspoon cayenne
2   tablespoons cilantro, chopped
2   cups water (or more)

Dough:
3   cups Laxmi brand flour (or whole wheat flour)
½   teaspoon salt
⅔   cup water (approximately)

Wash the tur dal twice.
In a medium-sized pot add the tur dal, 4 cups of the water and ½ teaspoon of turmeric. Bring to a boil and turn down until just boiling. Partially cover. Stir soup every 5 minutes or so to keep from sticking.
Add the rest of the water, cup by cup, as the soup thickens. Cook until tender, about an hour and a quarter. When cooked, cool slightly and beat smooth with an eggbeater.

While the dal is cooking, make the dough.
Mix the flour and salt together in a shallow bowl.
Add the ⅔ cup water, a little at a time, until you have a thick dough that does not stick to your hands. It is best to mix it with your hands. Knead for a few minutes. Cover the dough and set aside for 15 minutes or so.

recipe continues ➤

Heat a good-sized soup pot over a medium flame. Add the oil, mustard and cumin seeds. Stir or shake the pot until the seeds pop. Add the hing, the rest of the turmeric, salt, curry leaves, chili and cilantro and sauté a moment.
Add the cooked dal to the spices and enough water to make about 10 cups of "soup." Stir and bring this to a boil.

While the soup is coming to a boil, prepare the dough. Cut the ball of dough in half. Lightly flour a board and, with a rolling pin, roll each piece into a large chapati, ⅛ inch thick.
With the tip of a sharp knife, cut each chapati into 1 inch strips. Then cut across these strips on the diagonal every inch, making diamonds.

When the "soup" boils, add the diamonds, a few at a time. Bring back to a low boil and cook until the diamonds are cooked through, about half an hour. Stir occasionally. The diamonds are cooked when they feel soft when squeezed between thumb and finger, like a well-cooked noodle.
Serve for a main meal.

NOTE: It is very important to cook this well. Otherwise it will be difficult to digest.

Pitta can eat this in moderation. (See page 152 for more information about Laxmi flour.)

The chapati-like diamonds, when cooked in the dal, are something between a thick noodle and a dumpling. This dish is high in protein from the combination of dal and grain.

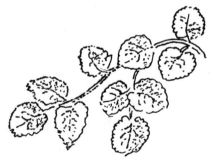

Fresh Cilantro

Urad Dal Soup

Serves 4

1   cups urad dal
5   cups water
1   tablespoon safflower oil
1   teaspoon black mustard seeds
1   teaspoon cumin seeds
4   curry leaves, fresh or dried
¼   cup fresh cilantro, chopped
2   cloves garlic, chopped
2   pinches cayenne pepper <u>or</u> 1 small green chili, chopped
1   pinch hing
¼   teaspoon turmeric
¾   teaspoon salt

Wash the urad dal twice.
Cook the urad dal in the water until tender, about half an hour. Stir occasionally.
Heat the oil in a large pot over medium heat. Add the mustard seeds, cumin seeds and curry leaves, and stir until the seeds pop.
Turn down the heat to low and add the cilantro, garlic, chili or cayenne and hing. Cook until the garlic is slightly brown. Add the cooked dal soup to the spices, then add the turmeric and salt.
Bring to a boil, turn off the heat and serve with rice and chapatis.

Urad dal is sweet, heavy, unctuous, and slightly heating. This is excellent, calming food for vata and they should eat it frequently. Pitta and kapha can eat it once or twice a week.
Urad dal soup detoxifies the system. It nourishes muscle, bone and reproductive fluids. It helps lactation and energizes the whole body.
This is not a good food for kapha disorders, especially obesity, nor for pitta disorders.
Never eat this soup with fish, yogurt or eggplant (all of these are heating), because it makes a bad food combination that can cause toxins.

Yellow Mung Dal Soup

Serves 6

1	cup yellow mung dal
6	cups water
4	tablespoons safflower oil
1	teaspoon black mustard seeds
1	teaspoon cumin seeds
1	pinch hing
2	large cloves garlic, chopped
1	small handful cilantro leaves, chopped
5	curry leaves, fresh or dried
½	teaspoon turmeric
1	teaspoon masala powder
¾	teaspoon salt

Wash the mung dal twice.

Put the mung dal and 3 cups of the water into a soup pot and bring to a boil. Cook on medium heat for 25 minutes, uncovered, stirring occasionally to prevent sticking.

Add the last 3 cups of the water and boil for another 20 minutes.

Remove from the heat and beat with an eggbeater until smooth. Set aside.

Heat the oil in a small saucepan until medium hot. Add the cumin seeds, mustard seeds and hing. Stir until the seeds pop.

Turn down the heat, add the garlic and brown lightly. Then put in the curry leaves, cilantro, turmeric and masala powder. Stir and add to the soup.

Add salt.

Boil for 2 minutes and serve.

Yellow mung is sweet and cooling, and mainly calms vata and pitta. It is very easy to digest and promotes strength.

The seasonings here help to balance the drying, light and astringent qualities of this soup that could aggravate vata.

Medicinal Uses: Good for fever, diarrhea, eye problems and skin conditions.

Kitcharis

Kitchari, a seasoned mixture of rice and mung dal, is basic to the Ayurvedic way of life. Basmati rice and mung dal both have the qualities of being sweet and cooling with a sweet after taste. Together they create a very balanced food, that is an excellent protein combination and is tridoshic. This complete food is easy to digest and gives strength and vitality. It nourishes all the tissues of the body. Kitchari is the preferred food to use when fasting on a mono-fast or while going through cleansing programs such as panchakarma. Kitchari is excellent for detoxification and de-aging of the cells. The proportions are usually 2 parts rice to 1 part of dal, but both these and the spices can be varied according to need and constitution.

The kitcharis that follow all have healing properties and they are all tridoshic.

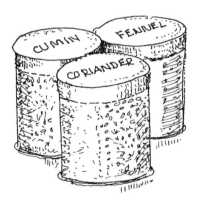

Mung Dal Kitchari (*Vata*)

Serves 4

1   cup basmati rice
½   cup yellow split mung dal
3   tablespoons ghee
1   teaspoon black mustard seeds
1   teaspoon cumin seeds
2   pinches hing
½   teaspoon turmeric
¾   teaspoon salt
4   cups water

Wash the rice and mung dal well. If you have time, let the mung dal soak for a few hours before cooking, as it helps with digestibility. If you have a particularly difficult time digesting beans, you may want to precook the beans for 20-30 minutes using the 4 cups of water.

In a saucepan over medium heat, heat the ghee and add the mustard seeds, cumin seeds and hing. Stir a moment until the seeds pop.

Add the rice, mung dal, turmeric and salt and stir until well blended with the spices.

Add the water and bring to a boil. Boil for 5 minutes, uncovered, stirring occasionally.

Turn down the heat to low and cover, leaving the lid slightly ajar. Cook until tender, about 20-25 minutes.

This kitchari can be eaten by all doshas but is especially good for vata.

Mung Dal Kitchari (*Pitta*)

Serves 6

1   cup yellow mung dal
1   cup basmati rice
1½ inch piece of fresh ginger, peeled and chopped fine
2   tablespoons unsweetened, shredded coconut
1   small handful cilantro leaves, chopped
½   cup water
3   tablespoons ghee
1   teaspoon black mustard seeds
1   teaspoon cumin seeds
1½ inch piece of a cinnamon stick
½   teaspoon turmeric
½   teaspoon salt
6   cups water

Wash the mung dal and rice two times. Soak the mung dal for a few hours, if you have the time, then drain.

Put the ginger, coconut, cilantro and the ½ cup water into a blender and blend until liquefied.

Heat the ghee on medium in a large saucepan and add the mustard seeds, cumin seeds, turmeric, salt, and cinnamon stick. Stir a moment until seeds pop. Then add the blended items. Stir well.

Next mix in the rice, mung dal and the 6 cups of water.

Bring to a boil. Boil, uncovered, for 5 minutes. Then cover, leaving the lid slightly ajar, turn down the heat to simmer and cook for 25 to 30 minutes, until the dal and rice are tender.

Although tridoshic, this kitchari is especially suitable to pitta. The cilantro and coconut add to the cooling qualities that pitta needs.

Mung Dal Kitchari (*Kapha*)

Serves 4 to 6

1   cup yellow split mung dal
1   cup basmati rice
3   tablespoons ghee
4   bay leaves
4   small pieces cinnamon bark
4   whole cloves
4   whole cardamom pods
6   cups water
¾   teaspoon salt

Wash the mung dal and rice twice. Soak the dal for a few hours, if you have time.

Heat a saucepan on medium and add the ghee. When it is hot, put in the bay leaves, cinnamon, cloves and cardamom and stir until the spices are mixed and fragrant.

Mix in the rice, dal, salt and water. Cook at a low boil, uncovered, for 5 minutes. Cover and cook on low heat until the dal and rice are soft, about 25-30 minutes.

This kitchari is tridoshic, but especially good for kapha because of the warming and pungent qualities of the spices.

Mung Dal Kitchari (*Tridoshic*)

Serves 4 to 5

1   cup yellow mung dal
1   cup basmati rice
1   inch piece of fresh ginger, peeled and chopped fine
2   tablespoons shredded, unsweetened coconut
1   small handful fresh cilantro leaves
½   cup water
3   tablespoons ghee
1½ inch piece of cinnamon bark
5   whole cardamom pods
5   whole cloves
10   black peppercorns
3   bay leaves
¼   teaspoon turmeric
¾   teaspoon salt
6   cups water

Wash the mung dal and rice until water is clear. Soaking the dal for a few hours helps with digestibility.

In a blender, put the ginger, coconut, cilantro and ½ cup water and blend until liquefied.

Heat a large saucepan on medium heat and add the ghee, cinnamon, cloves, cardamom, peppercorns and bay leaves. Stir for a moment until fragrant.

Add the blended items to the spices, then the turmeric and salt. Stir until lightly browned.

Stir in the mung dal and rice and mix very well.

Pour in the 6 cups of water, cover and bring to a boil. Let boil for 5 minutes, then turn down the heat to very low and cook, lightly covered, until the dal and rice are soft, about 25 - 30 minutes.

This kitchari is especially beneficial for tridoshic balancing.

Tapioca Kitchari (*Sabudana*)

Serves 4 to 5

3   cups tapioca (medium size is best)
2   cups peanuts (without skins and unsalted)
¾   cup ghee
1   teaspoon cumin seeds
1   small green chili, chopped
½   cup cilantro leaves, chopped
½   teaspoon salt

Wash the tapioca well, in lots of water, twice. Then drain it and set aside for 1 hour.
Dry roast the peanuts in a frying pan for 2-3 minutes, until slightly toasted. Grind them in a blender to a medium-fine powder, but <u>not</u> to the peanut butter stage. (Peanut butter is not a satisfactory substitute in this recipe.)
Heat a medium-sized pan and add the ghee and cumin seeds. Stir a moment until they pop.
Add the chili and cilantro, then the tapioca, ground nuts and salt.
Cook and stir on medium heat until the tapioca becomes soft, about 5-8 minutes. Turn down the heat to simmer and cover. Cook until the tapioca has a porridge-like consistency.

It may be a surprise to find that there is no water in this recipe. This allows the tapioca to keep its shape and be a bit crunchy. If water is added, a sticky pudding will result.

Tapioca is sweet, astringent and cooling with a sweet vipaka. It is a starchy food and especially good for fasting days. It calms pitta and kapha. It is an excellent food for breakfast, but should not be used for the main meal in a regular diet. Grains should not be eaten with tapioca.

The dry, light and astringent qualities of tapioca may stimulate vata, so they should reserve this kitchari for occasional use only.

Medicinal Uses: This is the best food for the patient of fever, diarrhea, poor digestion and weak intestines.

Mainly Rice Dishes

In Ayurveda, rice, especially basmati rice, is the most common grain in the diet. Ayurvedic cooking seldom uses brown rice, as it is more difficult to digest, too heating for pitta and too heavy for kapha. Rice is especially good for vata and pitta, and okay for moderate use by kapha.

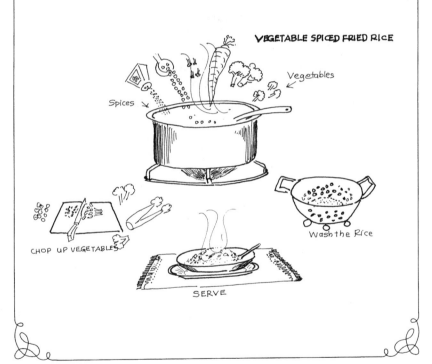

VEGETABLE SPICED FRIED RICE

Vegetables

Spices

CHOP UP VEGETABLES

Wash the Rice

SERVE

"Plain Rice"

Serves 4

2   cups basmati rice
1   tablespoon ghee
1   pinch cumin seeds
½   teaspoon salt
4   cups hot water

Wash the rice twice and drain.
To wash rice properly, put the measured rice in a saucepan and fill to the top with water. Stir and gently pour off the water until the rice starts to escape. Fill again with water and stir 2 or 3 times. Gently pour off the water and put the last of the rice and water through a colander to drain completely. Rinse the last grains of rice out of the pan into the colander.
Dry the saucepan on medium-low heat. Sauté the cumin seeds in the ghee for a moment, then stir in the rice. Mix very well.
Add the salt and hot water. Bring to a boil and boil for 2-3 minutes.
Turn down the heat to very low and cover. For stickier rice, leave the lid slightly ajar. For drier rice, leave the lid tight.
Cook until the rice is tender, about 15-20 minutes.

Plain Rice can be eaten with Lentil Soup, Kokam Soup or Mixed Vegetable Soup.

Plain rice is sweet and cooling with a sweet vipaka. It is hydrophilous (retains water) so may increase kapha if taken in large quantities. In moderation, it is balancing for all doshas.

Fried Rice

Serves 4

1   cup basmati rice
2½ cups water
½   teaspoon salt
3   tablespoons sunflower oil
½   teaspoon mustard seeds
½   teaspoon cumin seeds
1   pinch hing
1   pinch turmeric
½   large onion, cut lengthwise into fine strips
½   small green chili, chopped
7   curry leaves, fresh or dried
2   tablespoons cilantro, chopped

Wash the rice twice and drain.
To a medium pot, add the rice, water and salt. Bring to a boil. Partially cover and boil gently for 5 minutes. Turn down the heat to simmer, cover and cook until tender, about 15 minutes.
Heat a heavy frying pan on medium heat. Add the oil. When the oil is hot, add the cumin and mustard seeds. Stir a moment until the seeds pop. Add the rest of the spices and the onion. Sauté until the onions are translucent.
Add the cooked rice to the spices and onions. Stir quickly and serve.

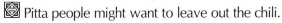 Pitta people might want to leave out the chili.

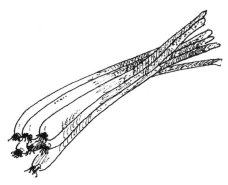

Saffron Rice

Serves 6

1   pinch saffron
1   tablespoon water
1½ cups basmati rice
3   tablespoons ghee or unsalted butter
4   bay leaves
7   bits of cinnamon bark (about 1 heaping teaspoon)
7   whole cloves
½ teaspoon salt
7   whole cardamom pods
4   cups of hot water

Soak the saffron in the I tablespoon water for at least 10 minutes.
Wash and rinse the rice twice. Drain.
Heat a pot over medium heat and add the ghee. Then add the bay leaves, cinnamon, cloves, salt and cardamom and mix well for a minute. Turn the heat to low, add the rice and sauté in the spices for 2 minutes.
Pour in the hot water and the soaked saffron and bring to a gentle boil. Boil uncovered for 5 minutes. Then turn down the heat to medium and partially cover.
Continue to boil gently for another 5 minutes, stirring once or twice to keep from sticking.
Turn the heat to low, fully cover and simmer until tender, about 10 minutes.

Saffron is sweet, astringent, and bitter to taste, heating with a sweet vipaka. It is balancing for all three doshas, easy to digest and helps food allergies.

Medicinal Uses: Very effective for migraine-type headache. It can be effective in revitalizing the blood, circulation and the female reproductive system.

Spicy Eggplant Rice

Serves 4 as a main dish

1   cup basmati rice
1½ inch piece of fresh ginger, peeled and chopped fine
2   tablespoons shredded coconut
1   small handful cilantro leaves
½   cup water
3   tablespoons ghee
1   teaspoon cumin seeds
1   teaspoon black mustard seeds
1   pinch hing
1   clove garlic
5   whole bay leaves
1   inch (about 1 teaspoon) cinnamon bark
5   whole cloves
6   curry leaves, fresh or dried
5   cardamom pods
1   teaspoon masala powder
¾   teaspoon salt
1   cup fresh eggplant, chopped in 1-inch sized pieces
3   cups hot water
    lime, coconut and cilantro for garnish

Wash the rice at least twice and drain. Wash and chop the eggplant.
Blend the ginger, coconut and cilantro in a blender with the ½ cup of water until liquefied. Set aside.
Heat a medium-sized pot over medium heat and add the ghee. When hot, add the cumin seeds, mustard seeds and hing. When the seeds pop, add the garlic and sauté until lightly browned.
Now add the bay leaves, cinnamon, cloves, curry leaves, cardamom, masala powder and salt. Mix well. Pour in the blended mixture. Stir and simmer for a minute. Mix in the rice and eggplant.
Pour in the 3 cups of hot water and bring to a boil. Boil for 2 minutes.
Turn down the heat to medium-low. Partially cover and cook at a low boil for 5 minutes, stirring occasionally.
Now turn the heat to low, cover and cook until tender, about 10-12 minutes.
Garnish with fresh cilantro, coconut and a lime wedge.

recipe continues ➤

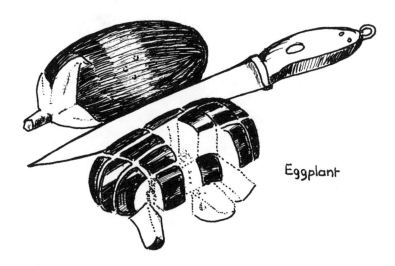 Eggplant can provoke pitta, so pitta types should eat this only occasionally, leaving out the garlic, clove and hing.

This dish is easy to digest, but still it should be eaten in moderation by vata and kapha.

Eggplant

Spicy Rice with Peas

Serves 4 to 5

2	cups basmati rice
1	cup fresh or frozen green peas
1	inch piece of fresh ginger, peeled and chopped fine
2	tablespoon unsweetened, shredded coconut
1	small handful fresh cilantro leaves
½	cup water
4	tablespoons ghee
1	teaspoon cumin seeds
1	teaspoon black mustard seeds
5	whole bay leaves
1½	inches cinnamon stick
7	cloves
7	cardamom pods
1	teaspoon masala powder
½	teaspoon salt
4	cups hot water
	cilantro, coconut and lime for garnish

Wash the rice and peas twice.

Blend the ginger, coconut, cilantro and the ½ cup water in a blender until liquefied. Set aside.

Heat a good-sized saucepan over medium heat and add the ghee, cumin seeds, mustard seeds and bay leaves. Stir until the seeds pop.

Then put in the cinnamon, cloves, cardamom, blended mixture, masala powder and salt. Sauté for 1 minute.

Mix in the rice and the peas. Stir well and add the 4 cups of hot water. Bring to a boil for 2 minutes. Turn down the heat, cover and cook, stirring occasionally, until tender, about 20 minutes.

Garnish with cilantro and coconut. Put a squeeze of lime on each individual serving.

Green peas are bitter, astringent and cooling, with a pungent after taste. The peas must be well cooked or they will ferment and cause gas.

Vata can eat this in small quantities with extra ghee.

Medicinal Uses: Well-cooked peas eliminate feces and gases from the colon.

Spicy Potato Rice

Serves 4 to 5

2   cups basmati rice
1   cup potatoes, peeled and chopped into 1 inch cubes
1½ inch piece of fresh ginger, peeled and chopped fine
1   small handful fresh cilantro leaves
2   tablespoons unsweetened, shredded coconut
½   cup water
4   tablespoons ghee
1   teaspoon cumin seeds
1   teaspoon black mustard seeds
5   whole bay leaves
1   inch piece cinnamon stick, broken up
7   whole cloves
7   cardamom pods
1   teaspoon masala powder
½   teaspoon salt
4   cups hot water
    lime wedges, cilantro, coconut for garnish

Wash the rice and chopped potato two times.
Put the ginger, coconut, cilantro and the ½ cup water in a blender and blend until liquid.
Heat a large saucepan on medium heat and add the ghee, then the cumin seeds, mustard seeds and bay leaves. Stir until the seeds pop.
Next add the cinnamon, cloves, cardamom, blended mixture, masala powder and salt. Sauté slightly for 1 minute.
Mix in the rice and potato and stir to coat with the spices.
Pour in the hot water and bring to a boil. Partially cover and boil for 12 minutes, then cover and cook over low heat for about 15 minutes.
Garnish with cilantro and coconut. Give each individual serving a squeeze of fresh lime.

Potatoes are nightshades so, in general, disturb the tridoshic balance. The spices help make the potatoes more digestible. This dish is very energizing.

The light and dry nature of potatoes provokes vata, so they should eat only a small quantity with extra ghee.

Spicy Vegetable Rice

Serves 4 to 6

2	cups basmati rice
½	cup zucchini, chopped
½	cup green beans, chopped
½	cup fresh peas
	(carrots, potatoes, cauliflower or broccoli may be added or substituted according to dosha)
3	cloves garlic, chopped
1	inch piece of fresh ginger, peeled and chopped fine
¼	cup fresh cilantro leaves
2	tablespoons shredded, unsweetened coconut
½	cup water
½	cup ghee
1	teaspoon cumin seeds
1	teaspoon black mustard seeds
¼	teaspoon turmeric
1	pinch hing
12	whole cloves
8	bay leaves
10	cardamom pods
2	inch piece of cinnamon stick, broken into small pieces
½	teaspoon salt
½	teaspoon cayenne or more to taste
5	cups of water
	lime, coconut and cilantro for garnish

Wash the rice twice and drain. Wash and chop the vegetables into bite-sized pieces.

Put the garlic, ginger, cilantro, coconut and the ½ cup water in a blender. Blend until liquid and set aside.

Heat a good-sized saucepan on medium and add the ghee, mustard seeds, cumin seeds, turmeric and hing. Cook for a moment until the seeds pop. Add the cloves, bay leaves, cardamom, cinnamon and cayenne. Mix well.

Pour in the blended mixture and salt and cook until slightly browned.

Stir in the rice and vegetables and mix well to coat with spices.

Pour in the water and bring to a boil for a few minutes. Cover loosely and turn down the heat to low. Cook until tender, about 15-20 minutes.

recipe continues →

Garnish with fresh lime, a sprinkle of chopped cilantro and coconut.

 This dish balances tridosha, because cooking the vegetables together gets rid of any individual aggravating qualities to a dosha.

For pitta, don't use the garlic, cayenne or cloves in the recipe. It will still taste good!

Cauliflower

Poha

Serves 4 to 5

3	cups poha (the thick kind)
⅓	cup safflower oil
1	teaspoon black mustard seeds
1	teaspoon cumin seeds
5	curry leaves, fresh or dried
½	teaspoon turmeric
½	teaspoon salt
1	pinch hing
½	cup cilantro leaves, chopped
1	small onion, chopped fine
1	small green chili, chopped fine
	coconut, cilantro and lime for garnish

Wash the rice flakes twice, drain and set aside.
Heat the oil in a frying pan, over medium heat, and add the mustard seeds, cumin seeds and curry leaves.
Stir until the seeds pop and put in the turmeric, salt and hing.
Next add the cilantro, onions and chili and cook until soft and slightly brown. Stir in the rice flakes, cover and turn off heat. Serve after a few minutes, garnished with coconut and cilantro. Give each serving a squeeze of fresh lime.

Poha is uncooked basmati rice that has been rolled thin in the same way that rolled oats are made. It cooks quickly and does not need water, other than what is absorbed in rinsing.

Poha is easy to digest and quite balancing for tridosha. It is a good breakfast food or can be used to accompany the main meal.

Poha with Potatoes

Serves 6

4	cups poha (the thick kind)
1	medium-sized potato, grated
6	tablespoons safflower oil
1	teaspoon cumin seeds
½	teaspoon mustard seeds
1	pinch hing
10	curry leaves, fresh or dried
1	small handful cilantro leaves, chopped
1	small green chili, chopped fine
1	small onion, chopped fine
1	teaspoon turmeric
1	handful of peanuts
½	teaspoon salt

Wash the poha twice and drain well. Set aside.

Wash and peel the potato. Grate it medium-fine.

Heat a frying pan on medium and add the oil. When hot, add the cumin seeds, mustard seeds, curry leaves and hing. Let the seeds pop. Then add the cilantro, green chili and onion.

Cook over medium heat until the onion is translucent, stirring constantly to keep from sticking.

Add the grated potato. Stir well again, cover and cook for 5 minutes. Stir, then cook for another 5 minutes.

Add the salt, turmeric, peanuts and the poha. Mix well. Cover, turn off heat and let sit for a few minutes.

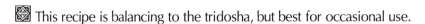 This recipe is balancing to the tridosha, but best for occasional use.

Vata should eat this in moderation because it tends to be hard to digest.

Murmura Chivda (*Snack Food*)

Serves a small crowd

14 cups murmura
1   cup whole peanuts
½   cup safflower oil
1   cup roasted dal
1   teaspoon black mustard seeds
1   teaspoon cumin seeds
2   pinches hing
1   teaspoon turmeric
1   green chili, chopped fine <u>or</u> ½ teaspoon cayenne
10 curry leaves, fresh or dried
1   small handful fresh cilantro leaves, chopped
1   teaspoon salt

Put the murmura in a large bowl and set aside.
Heat the oil in a deep frying pan until it is hot but not smoking. The oil is ready when a peanut dropped in bubbles quickly.
Add the peanuts and stir gently with a slotted spoon until very lightly browned, about 2-3 minutes. Remove from the oil, drain and add to the rice.
Now add the roasted dal to the hot oil, stir gently until lightly browned, about 2 minutes. Remove, drain and add to the murmura and peanuts.
Turn down the oil to medium-low and add the mustard seeds, cumin seeds, hing, chili, turmeric, curry leaves and cilantro. Stir and sauté for a moment, then sprinkle all of this, including any extra oil, over the murmura. Add salt if desired. Mix very well.

This amount serves a small crowd. Leftovers keep well when covered.

Both the murmura and roasted dal can be found in Indian grocery stores. Murmura is popped, unseasoned white rice.

Use cayenne instead of the chili for a less spicy mixture.

Tridoshic, but pitta should go easy on the hing, peanuts and mustard seeds.

Buttermilk Curry

Serves 4 to 6

2   tablespoons ghee
1   teaspoon black mustard seeds
1   teaspoon cumin seeds
1   pinch hing
4   curry leaves, fresh or dried
1   clove garlic, chopped
½   small green chili, chopped
1½ inch piece of fresh ginger, peeled and chopped fine
1   small handful fresh cilantro leaves, chopped
½   teaspoon turmeric
½   teaspoon salt
4   cups buttermilk (use goat milk for Kapha)

Heat the ghee in a saucepan over medium heat and add the mustard seeds, cumin seeds, curry leaves and hing. Stir until the seeds pop.

Add the garlic and chili and brown slightly. Then add the ginger, cilantro and salt.

Pour in the buttermilk. Clean the measuring cup with ¼ cup water and add to the pot.

Stir in the turmeric and heat until just hot, but not boiling.

Good served with rice and chapati.

⊠ Kapha should have this only occasionally and should increase the mustard seeds and hing.

"Not-So-Plain" Tofu

Serves 4

1   pound organic tofu (firm tofu works best)
½   cup ghee
1   teaspoon cumin seeds
1   teaspoon black mustard seeds
1   pinch hing
1   clove garlic, chopped
1   green chili, chopped fine
1   small handful cilantro, chopped
½   onion, chopped fine
¼   teaspoon turmeric
1   teaspoon salt

In a frying pan, heat the ghee on a medium flame and add the mustard seeds, cumin seeds and hing. Stir until the seeds pop.
Add the garlic, chili, onion, cilantro and turmeric. Cook until the onions are slightly brown.
Crumble in the tofu. Stir and sauté gently for a few minutes. Cover and let sit at the back of the stove for the tofu to absorb the spices.

▦ Tofu is astringent, cooling and sweet.

Vata should eat this in moderation. It is heavy to digest and may also stimulate kapha. Extra garlic and chili (and moderation) will help keep kapha calm.

Vegetables and Tofu

V↓ P↓ K↑

Serves 4 to 6

3-4 cups any vegetables (broccoli, yellow and green zucchini, asparagus, celery are especially good)
1 recipe for *Not-So-Plain-Tofu* (previous page)

Wash vegetables and chop coarsely.
Make *Not-So-Plain-Tofu* recipe and add the vegetables with the tofu. Stir thoroughly to coat them with the ghee and the spices. Sauté and shake for 5 minutes.
Turn off heat. Cover and set at the back of the stove until the vegetables are just barely tender and still crisp.

 Same qualities as previous recipe.

Louki

Upma

Serves 4

1   cup creamed wheat
½   cup safflower oil or *ghee*
1   teaspoon black mustard seeds
1   teaspoon cumin seeds
1   pinch hing
5   curry leaves, fresh or dried
½   teaspoon turmeric
1   small green chili, chopped fine
1   small onion, chopped
¼   cup cilantro leaves, chopped
½   teaspoon salt
3   cups water
    coconut and cilantro leaves for garnish

Roast the creamed wheat in a heavy, dry pan over a medium heat until slightly brown. Stir or shake frequently. Set aside in a bowl to cool.

Heat a saucepan on medium and add the oil or *ghee*, then the mustard and cumin seeds. When the seeds pop, add the other spices except for salt.

Stir in the onion, cilantro and chili and cook until the onion is browned.

Add the salt and water and bring to a boil. Stir in the roasted mush very slowly. Let boil for 1-2 minutes while stirring continuously to prevent lumps from forming.

Turn down the heat and cover. Cook for 3-5 minutes.

Garnish with coconut and chopped cilantro leaves.

Give each serving a squeeze of fresh lime.

Roasting removes the allergens, glutamine and other *kapha* qualities of the wheat.

Kapha can eat this in moderation if they increase the mustard seeds and chili. Creamed wheat is sweet, unctuous and cooling. It is good as a breakfast food or to accompany the main meal.

Creamed Wheat Porridge

Serves 4

½ cup ghee
1 cup creamed wheat
4 cups water
½ teaspoon ground cardamom
½ teaspoon ground cinnamon
1 clove, whole

Heat a pot on a medium heat and add the ghee. Next add the creamed wheat, stirring it constantly until lightly brown and fragrant.
Pour in the water and stir vigorously until lumps are dissolved and the porridge is soft.
Add the cardamom, cinnamon, and clove. Turn the heat to simmer and cover until ready to serve. Serve with milk and sweetener, if desired.

This is an excellent breakfast food.

Kapha should add ⅛ teaspoon of ginger powder, reduce the ghee and only eat this occasionally.

Vegetables

The preferred method of preparing vegetables in Ayurveda is either to sauté them slowly in ghee or oil and spices or to cook them with spices in a small amount of water. Ayurveda does not recommend eating raw vegetables in quantity, as they are heavy, rough and difficult to digest. Raw vegetables and salads are better eaten in hot weather rather than in winter, and preferably at the noon meal, when agni is high. When two or more vegetables are cooked together they tend to "learn how to get along together" and so some of their non-harmonious qualities that could cause a bad food combination will disappear.

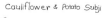
Cauliflower & Potato Subji

Bell Pepper Subji

Serves 4

4   cups bell peppers, chopped medium
2   tablespoons safflower oil
1   teaspoon cumin seeds
1   teaspoon black mustard seeds
1   pinch of hing
¼   teaspoon turmeric
½   teaspoon masala powder
2   tablespoons ground, roasted peanuts
2   tablespoons ground, roasted sesame seeds
½   teaspoon salt

Heat a frying pan on medium and put in the oil, cumin seeds, mustard seeds and hing. Stir until the seeds pop.

Add the turmeric, masala powder, ground peanuts, ground sesame seeds and salt. Stir, then add the chopped peppers. Turn down the heat to low and shake to mix well.

Cover and cook until the peppers are tender and soft, about 10 minutes.

Bell peppers are sweet, pungent and sour, a stimulant and a digestive.

This should be used in moderation by pitta and cooked without the hing and masala powder. Masala powder recipe is included in this book.

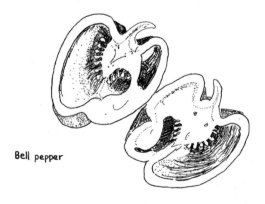

Bell pepper

Bitter Melon Subji No. 1

Serves 4

4   cups bitter melon
3   tablespoons safflower oil
1   teaspoon cumin seeds
1   teaspoon black mustard seeds
1   pinch hing
1   small handful cilantro leaves, chopped
3   cloves garlic, chopped
1½ inch piece of fresh ginger, peeled and chopped fine
1   small green chili, sliced in 4 pieces lengthwise
½   lime, quartered
¼   teaspoon turmeric
½   teaspoon salt

Cut the melon into round, bite-sized pieces.
Heat a shallow pot or frying pan on medium and add the oil, then the cumin seeds, mustard seeds and hing. Stir gently until the seeds pop.
Put in the melon, cilantro, garlic, ginger, chili and lime. Stir and add the turmeric and salt.
Shake to mix together and coat the melon. Cover and turn down the heat to low.
Cook until tender, about 25 minutes.

Bitter melon is bitter, cooling and pungent. It is light, easy to digest and calms kapha and pitta. This recipe balances the tridoshas—the cilantro calms pitta, the mustard seeds eliminate kapha and the safflower oil, cumin seeds and hing relieve vata. May provoke vata if eaten in excess.

Medicinal Uses: This is a good food for diabetes, anemia and for worms. It is a mild laxative and liver cleanser.

Bitter Melon Subji No. 2

Serves 4

3   tablespoons safflower oil
½   teaspoon cumin seeds
1   teaspoon black mustard seeds
1   pinch hing
4   cups bitter melon, cut in ⅛-inch crosswise slices
¼   teaspoon turmeric
½   teaspoon masala powder
¼   teaspoon salt
1   tablespoon ground, roasted peanuts
1   tablespoon ground, roasted sesame seeds

Heat a frying pan on medium and add the oil, cumin seeds, mustard seeds and hing.

Cook for a minute or two until the seeds pop and put in the turmeric, masala powder, salt, peanuts and sesame seeds. (Don't substitute peanut butter for the ground peanuts.) Mix well and add the melon.

Stir gently to coat the melon with spices.

Turn the heat to low and cook uncovered, stirring occasionally, until browned and crispy.

This has the same qualities as *Bitter Melon Subji No.1*. The peanuts help calm vata and give energy. It is a good food for skin diseases, diabetes and to clean the blood.

(KARELĀ) Bitter Melon

Cabbage Subji

Serves 4

1   medium head cabbage, chopped fine (approximately 6 cups)
2   tablespoons safflower oil
½   teaspoon black mustard seeds
½   teaspoon cumin seeds
1   piece cinnamon stick
2   cloves, whole
1   pinch hing
¼   teaspoon turmeric
½   small green chili, chopped fine
½   teaspoon salt

Wash the cut cabbage twice.

Heat a saucepan on medium heat and add the oil, mustard seeds, cumin seeds, hing, turmeric and green chili. Sauté until the seeds pop. Break the cinnamon stick into the pan.

Add the cabbage and salt. Stir and cover. Simmer on low heat until the cabbage is tender, but slightly crisp, about 8-10 minutes.

Can be eaten with rice and chapati or roti.

Cabbage is bitter, astringent, cooling and pungent. It is light, digestive and kindles gastric fire. Due to the binding and dry qualities, it can cause constipation and gas.

Although this recipe does balance tridosha, vata should eat it in moderation. The turmeric, hing and salt help alleviate the qualities that aggravate vata.

Medicinal Uses: Acts as a mild diuretic.

Carrot Subji

Serves 4

4   cups carrots, grated
1   small handful fresh cilantro, chopped
½   small green chili, chopped
1½ inch piece of fresh ginger, peeled and chopped fine
2   cloves garlic, chopped
2   tablespoons shredded, unsweetened coconut
½   cup water
1   tablespoon ghee
½   teaspoon black mustard seeds
½   teaspoon cumin seeds
1   pinch hing
½   teaspoon salt

Wash and grate the carrots medium fine.
Put the cilantro, chili, ginger, garlic, coconut and water in a blender and blend on high until liquid.
Heat a pot on medium and add the ghee, mustard seeds, cumin seeds and hing. When the seeds pop, add the blended mixture and salt and brown very slightly.
Stir in the carrots, cover and cook on medium heat until just tender, about 10 minutes. Stir occasionally.

⬛ Carrots have many qualities—sweet, bitter, pungent, heating, light, sharp. For pitta, go easy on the chili, garlic, mustard seeds and hing and eat in moderation. Cooked carrots are sweet and heating with a pungent vipaka, so this recipe is particularly balancing for vata and kapha.

Medicinal Uses: A good food for hemorrhoids, water retention and blood building. It is an excellent brain tonic and aids deep thinking.

Cauliflower and Potato Subji

Serves 4

4 cups mixed cauliflower and potato
1 medium-sized tomato, chopped
1½ inch piece of fresh ginger, peeled and chopped fine
2 tablespoons unsweetened, shredded coconut
¼ cup fresh cilantro leaves, chopped
½ cup water
5 curry leaves, fresh or dried
3 tablespoons safflower oil
1 teaspoon black mustard seeds
½ teaspoon cumin seeds
1 pinch hing
½ teaspoon masala powder
¼ teaspoon turmeric
¾ teaspoon salt
4 cups water

Wash the vegetables. Peel the potatoes. Cut the vegetables into bite-sized pieces.

Put the ginger, coconut, cilantro and the ½ cup water in a blender and mix until liquefied. Set aside.

Heat a deep frying pan on medium and add the oil, cumin seeds, mustard seeds and hing. Stir until the seeds pop. Then add the blended mixture, masala powder, turmeric and salt. Brown slightly and add the cauliflower, potato and tomato. Stir until all ingredients are mixed.

Pour in the 4 cups of water, cover and cook until just soft.

◈ Should be used in moderation by vata. The mustard seeds, hing and turmeric help take away the rough qualities of cauliflower.

Eggplant Subji

Serves 4

6 cups eggplant (about 2 medium-sized ones)
2 tablespoons safflower oil
1 teaspoon black mustard seeds
1 teaspoon cumin seeds
¼ teaspoon turmeric
1 pinch hing
1 medium onion, chopped fine
½ teaspoon masala powder
¾ teaspoon salt

Wash the eggplant and cut into ½ inch cubes.

Heat a saucepan on a medium flame and add the oil, mustard seeds, cumin seeds, turmeric and hing. Stir until the seeds pop.

Add the onion and cook until light brown and transparent.

Stir in the masala powder, salt and eggplant. Shake the pan until everything is thoroughly mixed. Cover and reduce the heat to low.

Cook until tender, about half an hour, and serve garnished with shredded coconut and chopped cilantro.

Eggplant is astringent, bitter, and heating, with a pungent vipaka. It aggravates pitta, but is generally balancing for vata and kapha.

Pitta can eat this occasionally if they leave out the hing, mustard seeds and masala.

Medicinal Uses: Kindles agni and detoxifies the colon, but should not be eaten by those with kidney and gallstone problems. Eggplant is a member of the nightshade family and high in oxalic acid, which may cause crystals.

Green Bean Subji

Serves 4

4 cups green beans, chopped
2 cloves garlic, chopped
1 inch piece fresh ginger, peeled and chopped fine
1 tablespoon shredded coconut
2 tablespoons fresh cilantro, chopped
⅓ cup water
2 tablespoons safflower oil
½ teaspoon cumin seeds
½ teaspoon black mustard seeds
¼ teaspoon turmeric
1 pinch hing
½ medium onion, chopped
½ teaspoon masala powder or cayenne
½ teaspoon salt

Snap off the ends of the beans and slice on the diagonal into very small pieces, about ¼ inch long. Wash the beans twice.

Purée the garlic, ginger, coconut, cilantro and water in a blender. Set aside.

Heat the oil in a medium saucepan. Add the cumin seeds, mustard seeds and hing.

When the seeds pop, add the turmeric, masala powder and chopped onion. Stir until the onion is soft and slightly brown.

Add the blended mixture, salt and green beans. Cover and simmer on low heat until just tender, about 5-10 minutes.

▨ Green beans are sweet, astringent, and cooling, with a pungent vipaka. They help kindle agni, but can disturb vata if eaten in excess. They have a tendency to produce gas and constipation.

Green beans alone will aggravate vata. The cumin seeds, hing and cayenne will help calm *vata*. But still *vata* should eat this in moderation.

Medicinal Uses: Good food for throat, lungs and pitta disorders.

Mixed Vegetable Subji

Serves 4

4   cups cut vegetables (green pepper, green beans, zucchini, yellow squash, etc.)
2   tablespoons ghee or safflower oil
½   teaspoon cumin seeds
½   teaspoon black mustard seeds
¼   teaspoon ajwan seeds
½   teaspoon masala powder or cayenne
¼   teaspoon turmeric
1   pinch hing
½   teaspoon salt

Wash, trim and cut the vegetables into bite-sized pieces. Try cutting each vegetable into a different shape for a nice visual effect.

Heat a deep frying pan on medium heat and add the oil or ghee, then the cumin seeds, mustard seeds, ajwan and hing.

When the seeds pop, add the masala or cayenne and turmeric. Stir briefly, then put in the vegetables and salt. Stir to coat them thoroughly with the spices. Turn down the heat to low and cover. Stir after 5 minutes.

Continue cooking on low for another 15 minutes or until the vegetables are just tender.

This subji has tridoshic energetics. It balances agni and is laxative. A good food for bones and joints.

ZUCCHINI

Okra Subji

Serves 4

1   pound fresh okra
1   tablespoon safflower oil
1   teaspoon cumin seeds
1   teaspoon black mustard seeds
½   green chili, chopped
½   teaspoon salt

Wash the okra and dry it. Trim off the top and bottom and cut into ¼-inch circles.
Heat the oil in a saucepan over medium heat and add the cumin and mustard seeds.
When the seeds pop, add the chili and salt. Stir until slightly brown.
Add the okra, cover and simmer until tender for 15 minutes. Stir often to avoid burning.

Okra is sweet, astringent, cooling and sweet. It is a very fine balancer for the three doshas. Okra is soft, slimy, and easy to digest when cooked.

Pitta should leave out the green chili. Also it is best to leave out the chili seeds for vata and kapha, as they are difficult to digest. The seeds are a gentle laxative.

Medicinal Uses: Lubricates joints. Good energizer and good for reproductive tissue. Excellent food for arthritis and osteoporosis.

Grated Potato Subji

Serves 4

4 cups white potatoes
2 tablespoons safflower oil
½ teaspoon black mustard seeds
½ teaspoon cumin seeds
1 pinch hing
½ small green chili, chopped
¼ teaspoon turmeric
¼ teaspoon ajwan
½ teaspoon salt

Wash, peel and grate the potatoes. Wash the grated potato and drain well. Heat a deep frying pan on medium and add the oil, mustard seeds, cumin seeds and hing. When the seeds pop, add the chili, turmeric, ajwan and salt. Stir and add the potatoes and mix well to coat with the spices.
Turn down the heat to low, cover and cook for 5 minutes. Stir, then cook for another 5 minutes.
Let it sit on the stove with the lid on and no flame for a few minutes and it will become more tender.

The hing, chili and ajwan help reduce the vata-aggravating qualities of the potato.

Pitta should not use the chilies and hing.

Potato Subji No. 1

Serves 4

3   medium potatoes
3   tablespoons safflower oil
1   teaspoon black mustard seeds
1   teaspoon cumin seeds
½   teaspoon ajwan seeds
¼   teaspoon turmeric
1   pinch hing
1   pinch cayenne
2   tablespoons cilantro leaves, chopped
½   teaspoon salt

Boil the potatoes in their skins until they are soft.
Drain and cool the potatoes, then skin and cut them into ½-inch cubes.
Heat a frying pan on medium and add the oil, then the mustard seeds, cumin seeds, ajwan and hing. Let the seeds pop.
Put in the turmeric, cilantro and cayenne. Stir and add the salt and potatoes.
Carefully mix the potatoes, coating them with the spices, and cook for 2-3 minutes on medium heat.

Vata can eat this occasionally. Pitta should go easy on the cayenne, ajwan and mustard seeds. Otherwise tridoshic.

Potato Subji No. 2

Serves 4

4	cups white potatoes
1	inch piece of fresh ginger, peeled and chopped fine
2	cloves garlic, chopped
2	tablespoons grated, fresh coconut (or dried)
1	small handful cilantro leaves, chopped
½	cup water
3	tablespoons safflower oil
½	teaspoon black mustard seeds
½	teaspoon cumin seeds
1	pinch hing
¼	teaspoon turmeric
¼	teaspoon ajwan
½	teaspoon masala powder or more to taste
4	curry leaves, fresh or dried
½	teaspoon salt
1	small tomato, coarsely chopped
4	cups water

Wash and peel the potatoes and cut them into 1 inch pieces. Rinse again.
Put the garlic, coconut, cilantro and the ½ cup water into a blender and blend until liquefied.
Heat a saucepan on medium and add the oil, then the mustard seeds, cumin seeds and hing. Stir until the seeds pop.
Add to the saucepan the turmeric, ajwan, curry leaves, blended mixture, masala powder and salt. Mix well and add the potatoes and tomatoes. Stir to coat them.
Add the 4 cups of water and bring to a boil. Turn down, partially cover and simmer until tender, about 20 minutes.

Pitta can eat this if they go easy on the garlic, ajwan and tomato. The seasonings will help vata digest the potatoes.

Potato Subji No. 3

Serves 4

4   cups white potatoes, peeled and diced in small cubes
3   tablespoons safflower oil
½   teaspoon black mustard seeds
½   teaspoon cumin seeds
1   pinch hing
¼   teaspoon ajwan
¼   teaspoon turmeric
½   teaspoon masala powder
1   medium onion, chopped fine
¼   teaspoon salt

Wash the cut potatoes twice.
Heat a frying pan on medium and add the oil, mustard seeds, cumin seeds, hing, ajwan and onion.
Sauté for a minute or two, then put in the turmeric, masala powder and salt. Stir until lightly browned.
Now add the potatoes, stirring gently until coated with the spices.
Cook, covered, on low heat until tender, stirring every 5 minutes to prevent sticking.

Tridoshic in moderation.

chopped onions

Spinach Subji

Serves 4

6   cups spinach, chopped and lightly packed
½   cup split yellow mung dal or tur dal
2   cups water
1   tablespoon safflower oil
1   teaspoon black mustard seeds
1   teaspoon cumin seeds
1   pinch hing
1   clove garlic, chopped
1   small green chili, chopped <u>or</u> ¼ teaspoon cayenne
½   teaspoon salt

Wash the spinach and the dal twice. Put them in a pot with the water and cook, uncovered, until tender, about 30 minutes. Tur dal may take longer. Beat the cooked dal and spinach slightly with an eggbeater and set aside. Heat a pan on medium and add the oil, then the cumin seeds, mustard seeds, hing, garlic, chili or cayenne. Cook until the garlic browns.
Pour in the cooked spinach and dal mixture. Add the salt and bring to a boil. Remove from the heat and serve.

🪷 Both vata and pitta can eat this once in awhile, but not often. Pitta should leave out the garlic.

Medicinal Uses: This is a good food for the lungs and detoxifies the blood, making it strong.

clove garlic

Squash Subji

Serves 4

2 tablespoons safflower oil
½ teaspoon cumin seeds
½ teaspoon black mustard seeds
1 pinch hing
4 curry leaves, fresh or dried
1 small handful fresh cilantro leaves, chopped
1 small green chili, chopped
4 cups any yellow winter squash
½ teaspoon salt
¼ teaspoon turmeric
1 cup water

Wash and peel the squash and cut into 1 inch cubes.
Heat a frying pan over medium heat and add the oil, then the cumin seeds, mustard seeds and hing. In a moment, when the seeds pop, add the curry leaves, cilantro, turmeric, chili and squash.
Sprinkle on the salt and add the water.
Stir or shake to mix well, partially cover and turn down the heat to low.
Cook until tender, about 25 minutes.

▨ Squash by itself is vata provoking, but cooked with the spices, it is all right for occasional use.

A good balancer for *pitta* and *kapha*.

White Radish Subji

Serves 4

4   cups white (daikon) radish, grated
2   tablespoons safflower oil
½   teaspoon black mustard seeds
½   teaspoon cumin seeds
¼   teaspoon turmeric
1   pinch hing
½   small green chili, chopped
½   teaspoon salt

Wash the radish and grate medium-fine. Rinse the grated radish twice.
Heat a frying pan on medium and add the oil, then the mustard seeds, cumin seeds, hing, turmeric, chili and salt.
Stir until the seeds pop. Add the radish and mix well.
Cover and cook on medium-low heat until tender, about 12 minutes. Excellent for digestion.

Radish is pungent and heating with a pungent vipaka. It is digestive and relieves gas.

Medicinal Uses: A good food for constipation, hemorrhoids and heart conditions. Radish has a diuretic action and is useful for kidney stones.

Black-eyed Pea Bhaji

Serves 4 to 6

1   cup black-eyed peas
8   cups water
1   large clove garlic, chopped
1   small handful fresh cilantro, chopped
1½   inch piece of fresh ginger, peeled and chopped fine
2   heaping tablespoons shredded, unsweetened coconut
½   cup water
2   tablespoons safflower oil
1   teaspoon black mustard seeds
1   teaspoon cumin seeds
1   pinch hing
5   curry leaves, fresh or dried
¼   teaspoon ajwan
¼   teaspoon turmeric
½-1 teaspoon masala powder or cayenne
¼   teaspoon salt

Soak the peas overnight. Wash them twice and drain.
Add the peas and 6 cups of the water to a large pot and cook over medium heat, uncovered, for 30 minutes.
Add the other 2 cups of water and cook for another 25 minutes or until the peas are tender. Set aside.
Put the garlic, cilantro, ginger, coconut and the ½ cup of water in a blender and blend on medium until liquefied. Set aside.
Heat a good-sized saucepan over medium heat. Add the oil, followed by the mustard seeds, cumin seeds, hing and curry leaves. When the seeds pop, stir in the blended coconut mixture. Next, add the ajwan, turmeric, masala or cayenne and salt. Cook and stir for 1 minute to lightly brown everything.
Pour in the peas and the cooking water, mixing well.
Rinse the blender with ½ cup of water and add to the soup.
Bring the soup to a boil and boil for 1 minute.

These peas are sweet, astringent, cooling and pungent. They are heavy to digest and may ferment in the intestines. Hing, cumin seeds and ajwan will help prevent this.
Vata can eat this occasionally if they increase the quantity of these three herbs.
Medicinal Uses: A good food for lactation.

Green Pea Bhaji

Serves 6

1   cup dried whole green peas
6-7 cups water
2   cloves garlic, chopped
1   small handful cilantro leaves, chopped
1½ inch piece of fresh ginger, peeled and chopped fine
1   heaping tablespoon unsweetened, shredded coconut
½   cup water
2   tablespoons safflower oil
1   teaspoon cumin seeds
1   teaspoon black mustard seeds
1   pinch hing
4   curry leaves, fresh or dried
½   teaspoon ajwan
½   teaspoon turmeric
½   teaspoon masala powder or more
½   teaspoon salt

Wash the peas and soak overnight. When ready to use, drain and discard this soaking water. Pick over and discard any small hard peas.
Add the peas and 4 cups of the water to a medium pot and cook over medium-high heat, uncovered, for 30 minutes.
Add 2 more cups of water and cook until tender, another 35-40 minutes.
Put the garlic, cilantro, ginger, coconut and the ½ cup of water into a blender and blend until liquefied.
Heat a saucepan and add the oil, mustard seeds, cumin seeds, hing and curry leaves. Cook a moment until the seeds pop, then add the blended coconut mixture, the ajwan, turmeric, masala powder and salt.
Stir and mix for a minute and pour in the cooked peas and liquid. If the bhaji is too thick, rinse out the blender with the last cup of water and stir it into the bhaji.
Bring to a boil for one minute, cover and turn off.

Green peas are astringent, bitter, cooling and pungent. Vata can eat them occasionally. This is a balancing food for the other two doshas, laxative and energizing.

Kidney Bean Bhaji

Serves 6

1 cup dried kidney beans
6-7 cups water
2 cloves garlic, chopped
1 inch piece fresh ginger, peeled and chopped fine
1 small handful fresh cilantro leaves, chopped
1 heaping tablespoon shredded, unsweetened coconut
½ cup water
4 tablespoons safflower oil
1 teaspoon black mustard seeds
1 teaspoon cumin seeds
1 pinch hing
5 curry leaves, fresh or dried
½ teaspoon ajwan
½ teaspoon turmeric
½ teaspoon masala powder
½ teaspoon salt

Soak the kidney beans overnight, then wash them twice. Drain them and discard the water.

Add 4 cups of the water and the beans to a soup pot and cook over medium heat, uncovered, for 30 minutes.

Then add the other 2 cups of water and continue cooking, uncovered, for 30-40 minutes or until the beans are tender.

Put the ginger, garlic, cilantro, coconut and the ½ cup of water in a blender and blend on medium until liquefied.

Heat a medium saucepan until hot, then add the oil, mustard seeds, cumin seeds, hing and curry leaves. Let the seeds pop, then stir in the blended mixture, followed by the ajwan, turmeric, masala powder and salt. Cook and stir for 1 minute, until slightly brown.

Add the beans and their cooking water to the spices. Mix well.

If the bhaji is too thick, rinse out the blender with the last cup of water and add this to the soup.

Boil for 1 minute and serve. Garnish with cilantro and coconut.

▨ This dish is balancing for tridosha, but pitta should not use the garlic and kapha should use it in moderation. The hing, garlic and ajwan help vata and kapha digest the beans.

Lima Bean Bhaji

Serves 4

½ inch piece of fresh ginger, peeled and chopped fine
1 clove garlic, chopped
1 small handful cilantro leaves
2 tablespoons shredded, unsweetened coconut
½ cup water
2 tablespoons safflower oil
1 teaspoon black mustard seeds
1 teaspoon cumin seeds
1 pinch hing
½ teaspoon turmeric
1 pinch cayenne
½ teaspoon masala powder
½ teaspoon salt
1½ cups fresh (or frozen) lima beans
2 cups water

Put the ginger, garlic, cilantro, coconut and the ½ cup of water in a blender and blend until smooth.

Heat a saucepan over medium heat, add the oil and then the mustard seeds, cumin seeds and hing. Stir until the seeds pop.

Next add the turmeric and masala powder. Sauté a moment and add the blended coconut mixture, stirring until slightly brown.

Now put in the beans and stir them gently until well coated with the spices. Add the salt and water. Bring to a boil.

Cover and turn down the heat to medium. Cook until tender, about 12-15 minutes. Drain and serve.

Vata can add a little more cayenne, masala and oil to help with digestion, and eat this dish in moderation.

Mung Dal and Vegetable Bhaji

V↓ P↓ K↓

Serves 4 to 6

2	cups total, green beans, broccoli, zucchini, carrots, potatoes, or eggplant, according to *dosha* (use 1 or several vegetables)
2	cups yellow split mung dal
5	cups water
1	tablespoon safflower oil
1	teaspoon cumin seeds
½	teaspoon black mustard seeds
1	small handful fresh cilantro, chopped
2	cloves garlic, chopped
1	pinch hing
¼	teaspoon turmeric
½	teaspoon salt
½	teaspoon masala powder or cayenne

Wash and prepare the vegetables by chopping into bite-sized pieces. Wash the mung dal.

In a saucepan, put the dal, vegetables and water. Cook, partially covered, until the dal and vegetables are tender, about 30 minutes. Stir frequently to keep from sticking.

Heat the oil on medium in a good-sized pot and add the mustard and cumin seeds. Stir until the seeds pop, then mix in the cilantro, garlic and hing. Cook until the garlic is slightly brown.

Add the mung dal mixture to the spices. Stir in the turmeric, salt and masala powder.

Bring to a boil, turn off the heat and serve.

(BAINGAN) Eggplant

Spicy Sautéed Asparagus

Serves 4

2   cups (or about ¾ pound) asparagus
1   tablespoon *ghee*
1   pinch black mustard seeds
1   pinch cumin seeds
1   pinch cayenne
1   pinch salt

Clean the asparagus well and remove the tough ends. Cut across the spears once, cutting them in half.
Heat a shallow saucepan and put in the *ghee*, mustard seeds, cumin seeds and cayenne. Let the seeds pop and add the asparagus and salt.
Sauté, stirring gently, for 4-5 minutes.
Cover, take off the heat and let it sit on the back of the stove for a few minutes.

Asparagus is astringent, sweet, cooling and a diuretic. It is balancing, tridoshic and mildly laxative. Vata can add a little more cayenne, pitta more cumin seeds and kapha more mustard seeds.

Stuffed Bitter Melon

V↑ P↓ K↓

Serves 4

2   bitter melons
2   cloves garlic, chopped very fine
1   small handful cilantro, chopped
1½ inch piece of fresh ginger, peeled and chopped fine
2   heaping tablespoons shredded, unsweetened coconut
½   cup water
2   tablespoons ground, roasted peanuts
2   tablespoons ground, roasted sesame seeds
½   teaspoon masala powder
¼   teaspoon turmeric
½   teaspoon salt
3   tablespoons safflower oil
½   teaspoon black mustard seeds
½   teaspoon cumin seeds
1   pinch hing
1   cup water

Wash and dry the melons. Cut off the ends. Cut each melon in half across the center. On each of these halves, cut across lengthwise, down to within ½ inch of the bottom, so that the four sections can be spread apart for stuffing. Be careful not to cut right through the melon.
Put the garlic, cilantro, ginger, coconut and the ½ cup of water into a blender and blend until liquid.
Pour the blended mixture into a bowl and add the ground peanuts and sesame seeds, then the masala powder, turmeric and salt. Mix well.
Now gently open up each cut piece of melon and stuff it with this mixture. Use your hands, as it is quite juicy.
Heat a shallow pan on medium heat. Add the *ghee*, mustard seeds, cumin seeds and hing. When the seeds pop, add the stuffed melons and any of the stuffing sauce that is left.
Rinse the blender with the cup of water and add to the melons.
Cook over medium-low heat, partially covered, until the melons are tender to the touch, about 20-25 minutes. Baste occasionally.

▨ Bitter melon is bitter and cooling, and the vipaka is pungent. It is juicy and light to digest. It may stimulate vata, so they should add a bit more hing, salt and roasted sesame seeds for balance.

Stuffed Yellow Chilies

Serves 4

½ pound of yellow chilies (2-inch size)
½ cup roasted and ground peanuts
½ cup roasted and ground sesame seeds
2 tablespoons unsweetened, shredded coconut
1 tablespoon fresh cilantro leaves, chopped
¼ cup water
3 tablespoons safflower oil
½ teaspoon black mustard seeds
½ teaspoon cumin seeds
¼ teaspoon salt
¼ teaspoon turmeric
1 pinch hing

Wash and dry the chilies. Cut one side of each chili lengthwise from just below the cap to the tip, making a pocket. Scrape out the seeds if you want a milder dish.

Into a blender, put the ground peanuts and sesame seeds, the coconut, cilantro and water. Blend on low into a thick paste.

Carefully stuff the chilies with this paste.

Heat a frying pan on medium and add the oil, then the mustard seeds, cumin seeds, salt, turmeric and hing. Sauté until the seeds pop.

Add the stuffed chilies. Fry on medium heat, turning gently and frequently on all sides, until the skins are evenly brown and the chilies are tender.

These chilies are medium-hot to the taste, except for the seeds near the stem which are very hot.

▨ Chilies are pungent and hot, sharp, penetrating and a stimulant. They are a good digestive and kindle agni.

Pitta can eat this dish occasionally by adding more coconut, cilantro and cumin seeds.

Stuffed Okra

Serves 4

1	pound of fresh okra
½	cup ground, roasted sesame seeds
½	cup ground, roasted peanuts
2	tablespoons unsweetened, shredded coconut
¼	teaspoon turmeric
½	teaspoon masala powder
1	pinch hing
¼	teaspoon salt
1	tablespoon fresh, chopped cilantro leaves
1	tablespoon chickpea flour
¼	cup water
3	tablespoons safflower oil
½	teaspoon cumin seeds
½	teaspoon black mustard seeds

Wash the okra, wipe dry and cut off the ends. Make a slice lengthwise from top to bottom on one side of each okra with the sharp point of a knife, making a pocket.

Mix together the sesame seeds, peanuts (do not substitute peanut butter), coconut, turmeric, masala powder, hing, cilantro, salt, chickpea flour and water into a paste. It is easiest to use your hands for this.

Open up the pocket in the cut okra and stuff it with this paste.

Heat a frying pan on medium heat and put in the oil, cumin and mustard seeds. Cook until the seeds pop.

Put in the okra and fry on medium heat, turning gently until they are browned and crispy, about 10 - 15 minutes.

Okra is tridoshic and laxative. Pitta might want to increase the amount of cilantro and coconut. Vata and kapha can increase the mustard seeds.

Stuffed Tomatoes

Serves 4 to 5

9	small (about 2 inch) tomatoes or Italian tomatoes
1	inch piece of fresh ginger, peeled and chopped fine
2	cloves garlic
1	handful fresh cilantro leaves
2	tablespoons unsweetened, shredded coconut
½	cup water
1	cup, roasted and ground peanuts
¼	teaspoon turmeric
½	teaspoon masala powder
½	teaspoon salt
2	tablespoons Sucanat or other natural sugar
2	tablespoons safflower oil
½	teaspoon black mustard seeds
½	teaspoon cumin seeds
1	pinch hing
2	cups water

Wash the tomatoes. Cut each one lengthwise from the tip to ½ inch from the stem and cut again lengthwise across this cut, forming a cross (+). Be careful not to cut right through the tomato.

Put the ginger, garlic, cilantro, coconut and the ½ cup of water in a blender and blend until liquefied.

Mix together the blended mixture, peanuts, turmeric, masala powder, salt and sugar to make a thick paste. Using your hands makes this easier.

Spread open the tomatoes and stuff each one with the nut paste, using your hands.

Heat a deep frying pan on medium and add the oil, cumin seeds, mustard seeds and hing. Stir until the seeds pop.

Put in the tomatoes and stir very gently.

Add the 2 cups of water and bring to a boil. Turn down the heat to low and partially cover. Cook until tender, about 10 minutes.

▨ Tomatoes, being nightshades, usually have a negative effect on the tridoshic balance, if taken in excess. The seasonings in the recipe above help ease this negative effect.

Vata can add some garlic and should eat this only occasionally.

Potato Vadha

Serves 4 to 5

5   white potatoes
1   green chili, chopped
1½   inch piece of fresh ginger, peeled and chopped fine
½   cup water
1   teaspoon cumin seeds
½   teaspoon turmeric
1   pinch hing
½   teaspoon ajwan seeds
1   teaspoon sesame seeds
½   teaspoon salt
1   small handful cilantro, chopped

Batter:
1½   cups chickpea flour
½   teaspoon turmeric
¼   teaspoon ajwan seeds
1   pinch baking soda
¾   cup water (approximately)
     oil for deep frying

Boil the potatoes in their skins. Drain, cool, peel and mash them.
Put the chili, ginger and the ½ cup of water in a blender, mix until liquid.
Sprinkle the spices, seeds, salt and cilantro on the mashed potatoes. Add the
blended mixture and mix well. Your hands will do the best job of mixing.
Form this potato mixture into patties, approximately 2 inches across and ½
inch thick, by rolling into balls and flattening them with your hands.
Now make the batter by adding the turmeric and ajwan to the chickpea flour
and mixing well. Then add the water a little at a time, stirring vigorously, until
you have a medium-thick paste. Gently mix in the baking soda. Set aside for
5-10 minutes.
In a heavy saucepan or deep frying pan, heat the oil until a drop of the batter
floats up instantly to the top.
Dip the potato patties into the batter, drain a little, and drop carefully into the
hot fat until the surface is covered.

recipe continues →

Fry, turning frequently, until each potato patty is a lovely golden brown color, about 5 minutes.

Eat with Coconut or Mint Chutney. Good for lunch or as a picnic food.

 Chickpea flour has a very grainy texture and is available from Indian grocery stores. Whole wheat flour is not a satisfactory substitute because the texture is very different.

Potatoes tend to provoke vata, so vata people should use extra hing and ajwan. Pitta might want to increase the cumin seeds and cilantro, and kapha add some chili and turmeric.

Kapha should eat this in moderation.

Samosas

Serves 4

Filling

4	medium-sized potatoes (about 2 cups)
2	cups mixed vegetables (carrots, fresh green peas, cauliflower are especially good)
1	handful cilantro, finely chopped
1	teaspoon coriander, ground
1	teaspoon cumin, ground
¼	teaspoon cinnamon, ground
½	teaspoon turmeric
½	teaspoon salt
½	teaspoon cayenne

Dough

3	cups all-purpose flour
¼	cup safflower oil
½	teaspoon salt
¾	cup water (approximately)
	oil for deep frying

Filling:

Wash the potatoes and boil whole in their skins until tender.

Wash the vegetables and chop very finely. Cook with a small amount of water until just tender.

When the potatoes are cooked, cool, then peel them and chop into small cubes.

Drain the cooked vegetables. Mix them with the potatoes. Add the cilantro, coriander, cumin, cinnamon, turmeric, salt and cayenne and mix well.

Dough:

Mix the flour and salt together in a shallow dish.

Heat the ¼ cup safflower oil until a speck of flour sizzles in it.

Make a "bowl" or depression in the flour. Pour the hot oil into the flour "bowl." Carefully mix well with your hands.

Now add the water, a few spoonfuls at a time, mixing and kneading with your hands until the dough is thick, smooth and not sticky.

Cover the dough and set it aside for 20 minutes or so.

recipe continues ➔

Assembling the samosas:

Break off a walnut-sized piece of the dough and make it into a ball. Roll this out on a lightly floured board until it is a circle, 4-5 inches across and about ⅛ thick.

Place about 2 tablespoons of the cooled filling in the center of the circle. Now cover the filling by folding over the edges, one-third at a time, to create a triangular shape. Pinch all the edges together very well. If they don't appear to be sticking, moisten them slightly with a bit of water or milk, then pinch. When all the samosas have been stuffed, begin to deep fry them. Heat the oil until a drop of dough sizzles to the surface. Place 1 or 2 samosas in the hot oil and deep fry them for about 4-5 minutes, turning them frequently until they are a soft golden color.

Drain on absorbent paper and serve with Mint Chutney.

▨ Kapha should eat these in moderation, because of the frying.
Same qualities as Potato Vadha.

Green Peas

Fresh Cilantro Pakora

Serves 4

4   cups fresh cilantro
2   cups chickpea flour
1   teaspoon ajwan seeds
½   teaspoon turmeric
1   pinch hing
½   teaspoon cayenne
½   teaspoon salt
¼   cup water
2   pinches baking soda
      oil for deep frying

Discard the larger stems from the cilantro. Wash and pat the leaves dry. Put them in a shallow bowl.
Add all the spices to the flour and mix well. Add half of the flour to the cilantro and mix well to coat the cilantro. Your hands will do the best job of mixing. Put in the rest of the flour and stir and toss well.
Now add the water, a bit at a time, mixing constantly with your hands until you have a thick, sticky paste.
Sprinkle the baking soda over this paste and mix lightly.
Set aside for 15-20 minutes.
Heat oil for deep frying, until a drop of pakora mixture instantly floats to the top. Don't let the oil smoke.
Drop a teaspoon-sized amount of pakora mix into the oil until the surface is covered. Using a teaspoon gives a dumpling shape to the pakora, whereas dropping the dough from your fingers gives a more delicate, interesting shape. Stir and turn the pakoras until they are lightly brown on all sides, about 4-5 minutes. Drain and serve warm.

Cilantro is astringent, sweet and cooling with a sweet vipaka. It is light and especially calming to pitta. This recipe is tridoshic.

Kapha should eat this in moderation.

Onion Pakora

V↓↑ P↑ K↑↓

Serves 2 to 3

1 large onion
1¼ cups chickpea flour
1 teaspoon ajwan
½ teaspoon turmeric
¼ teaspoon cayenne
1 pinch hing
2-3 tablespoons water
2 pinches baking soda
½ teaspoon salt
   oil for deep frying

Cut the onion in half lengthwise, then slice lengthwise again into long, thin slices.

Add the spices and salt to the flour, mix well and sprinkle half of this onto the cut onions. Stir well, preferably with your hands, to coat the onion. Add the rest of the flour, mixing well.

Now sprinkle in the water, drop by drop, mixing constantly with your hands, until there is a thick, sticky paste around the onions.

Sprinkle the baking soda over this paste and mix lightly.

Set aside for about 10 minutes.

Heat oil for deep-frying until a drop of pakora dough floats instantly to the top. Don't let the oil smoke.

Select the individual pieces and carefully drop them into the oil until the surface is covered. Turn and stir until the pakoras are light brown in color, about 4-5 minutes. Drain and serve warm.

Pakora

▨ Raw onion is pungent, heating, pungent, and heavy to digest. Kapha can add some cayenne pepper to make it more calming and only eat it occasionally.

Medicinal Uses: Cooked onions are very effective for regulating vata disorders.

Spinach Pakora

Serves 4

4   cups fresh spinach
2   cups chickpea flour
1   teaspoon ajwan seeds
½   teaspoon turmeric
1   pinch hing
½   teaspoon cayenne
½   teaspoon salt
¼   cup water
2   pinches baking soda
    oil for deep frying

Remove the stems from the spinach. Wash, shake dry and chop medium fine. Add all the spices to the flour and mix well. Add half of the flour to the spinach and mix well to coat the spinach. Your hands will do the best job. Put in the rest of the flour and stir and toss well.

Now add the water, a bit at a time, mixing constantly with your hands until you have a thick, sticky paste.

Sprinkle the baking soda over this paste and mix lightly.

Set aside for 15-20 minutes.

Heat oil for deep frying, until a drop of pakora mixture instantly floats to the top. Don't let the oil smoke.

Drop teaspoon-sized amounts of pakora mix into the oil until the surface is covered. Using a teaspoon gives a dumpling shape to the pakora, whereas dropping the dough from your fingers gives a more delicate, interesting shape. Stir and turn the pakoras until they are lightly brown on all sides, about 4-5 minutes. Drain and serve warm.

Cooked spinach is astringent, sour, and heating with a sweet vipaka. By itself is stimulating to pitta but pacifying to vata and kapha if used in moderation. It is heavy to digest and can have a laxative effect. If vata adds extra hing, salt and a pinch of ajwan, and kapha extra turmeric and cayenne, then they can eat this occasionally.

Spinach should be avoided by those with kidney or gallstones.

Vegetable Pakora

Serves 4 to 6

Any vegetables, according to your constitution, can be used here, to a total of 4 cups, such as:
-green peppers, cut crosswise into ¼ inch slices
-white radish, cut thinly crosswise
-mushrooms, sliced lengthwise into ¼ inch slices
-zucchini, sliced thinly crosswise into ⅓ inch pieces
-large green chilies, cut lengthwise to 1 inch from stem
-potato, white or sweet, cut into thin slices

½ teaspoon cumin seeds
¼ teaspoon ajwan seeds
¼ teaspoon salt
¼ teaspoon turmeric
½ teaspoon cayenne
3 cups chickpea flour
2 pinches baking soda
1 cup water
  oil for deep frying

Mix the flour, spices and salt well.
Work in ½ cup of the water and mix until smooth. Then add the rest of the water, mixing well, until it is like a medium-thick pancake batter. Mixing with your hands works best for this.
Mix in the baking soda. Cover and let sit for 20-30 minutes.
Wash, dry and prepare the vegetables.
Heat the oil in a heavy, deep frying pan until a drop of the batter sizzles.
Dip each piece of vegetable into the batter, shake slightly, then drop into the oil until the surface is covered. Turn frequently with a slotted spoon until golden brown, 3-6 minutes, depending on the vegetable.

This is a balancing recipe, but pitta should add extra cumin seeds, kapha extra cayenne and vata extra ajwan.

Kapha can eat this occasionally.

Raitas

Raita is a tasty condiment to accompany your meals and is a good aid to digestion. Yogurt is the main ingredient in all raitas. By itself yogurt is sour, heating and difficult to digest. The spices in the following recipes help make yogurt more digestible. Most important, yogurt should be eaten in very small quantities, a spoonful or two with a meal. Ayurveda does not suggest eating yogurt by the bowl, except in certain health conditions.

CARROT RAITA

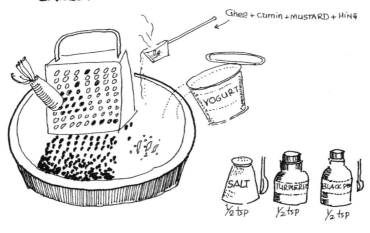

Ghee + cumin + MUSTARD + HING

YOGURT

SALT ½ tsp
TURMERIC ½ tsp
BLACK PEPPER ½ tsp

Beet Raita

Serves 4 to 6

1   cup raw beets, peeled and grated
2   tablespoons ghee
½   teaspoon black mustard seeds
½   teaspoon cumin seeds
1   pinch hing
1   tablespoon cilantro, chopped
½   small green chili <u>or</u> 1 large pinch cayenne
5   curry leaves, fresh or dried
1   cup plain yogurt
¼   teaspoon salt

Add the beets to the yogurt and stir gently.
Heat the ghee on medium heat in a saucepan. Add the mustard seeds, cumin seeds and hing. Stir until the seeds pop. Add the cilantro, curry leaves and chili or cayenne. Mix quickly and take off the stove. Cool a little and add to the yogurt and beets. Mix well.

Serves 4-6 as a side dish with meal, 1 or 2 spoonfuls per person

⬚ Beets, also known as beetroot, are sweet, cooling and have a pungent vipaka. The pungency may aggravate pitta, but occasional use is okay, especially with something pitta-pacifying such as cilantro. Kapha can eat this occasionally.
The spices in this recipe help lighten the heavy quality of the yogurt.

Beets are a good blood tonic and blood builder.

Carrot Raita

Serves 6 to 8

1   cup raw carrots
½   green chili, chopped fine
2   tablespoons ghee
½   teaspoon black mustard seeds
½   teaspoon cumin seeds
1   pinch hing
1   small handful cilantro leaves, chopped
1   cup plain yogurt
¼   teaspoon salt

Wash the carrots and grate medium fine.
Stir the carrots into the yogurt and mix gently.
Heat the ghee in a small saucepan and add the mustard seeds, cumin seeds and hing. Stir until the seeds pop, then add the chili and cilantro. Remove from the heat.
Mix the cooked spices and the salt into the yogurt/carrot mixture.

Serves 6-8 as side dish, a spoonful or two per person

▨ The pungent and heating qualities of carrots may provoke pitta.
Occasional use is okay for pitta, if they add extra cumin seeds and cilantro.
Kapha can eat this occasionally.

It is not wise to eat carrots too frequently during pregnancy.

Cucumber Raita

V↓ P↓ K↑

Serves 4 to 6

2 cucumbers
3 tablespoons ghee
½ teaspoon black mustard seeds
½ teaspoon cumin seeds
1 pinch of hing
4 curry leaves, fresh or dried
½ teaspoon salt
1 small handful cilantro leaves, chopped
1 pinch cayenne <u>or</u> ½ small chili, chopped
½ cup plain yogurt

Skin and grate the cucumbers. Pour off and discard any excess juice.
Heat the ghee in a saucepan over medium heat and add the mustard seeds,
cumin seeds, hing, curry leaves, and salt. Cook a moment until the seeds pop.
Add the cayenne or chili and cilantro, shake and take the pan off the heat.
Stir the yogurt and grated cucumber together in a bowl.
Add the cooled spices to the yogurt mixture, mix well and serve.

Serves 4-6 as side dish, 1 or 2 spoonfuls per person

▧ Cucumber is cooling and sweet but the skin is bitter.

Both the cucumber and the yogurt in this recipe can provoke kapha. Kapha
can eat this occasionally, with extra hing and mustard seeds.

Jalapeño Chilies

Spinach Raita

Serves 4 to 6

1 large bunch raw spinach (about 4 cups)
2 tablespoons ghee
½ teaspoon black mustard seeds
½ teaspoon cumin seeds
1 pinch hing
4 curry leaves, fresh or dried
2 tablespoons cilantro leaves, chopped
1 large pinch cayenne
½ cup ground, roasted peanuts (not peanut butter)
¼ teaspoon salt
1 cup plain yogurt

Remove the stems, wash and chop the spinach finely.
Heat the ghee in a saucepan on medium-high heat. Add the mustard seeds, cumin seeds, curry leaves and hing. Cook gently until the seeds pop.
Add the cilantro and cayenne and remove from the heat.
In a bowl, gently mix the spinach and yogurt, peanuts and salt. Then add the cooled spices, stir and serve.

Serves 4-6 as side dish, 1 or 2 spoonfuls per person

▨ The spices in this recipe will help to alleviate some of the rough and cooling qualities of spinach, but vata and pitta should still take it only occasionally and when needed for medicinal use. As we have seen in other recipes, spinach is a blood cleanser. It shouldn't be taken by those with kidney or gallstones.

Tomato Raita

Serves 8 to 10

4   cups fresh tomatoes, chopped
1   cup yogurt
2   tablespoons ghee
½   teaspoon cumin seeds
½   teaspoon black mustard seeds
1   pinch hing
5   curry leaves, fresh or dried
1   small handful cilantro, chopped
1   large pinch cayenne <u>or</u> ½ small green chili, chopped
¼   teaspoon salt

Wash and chop the tomatoes, medium fine.
Gently mix the tomatoes and yogurt and set aside.
Heat a small pan on medium heat and put in the ghee. When hot, add the mustard seeds, cumin seeds, hing and curry leaves. Stir until the seeds pop. Add the cilantro and cayenne or chili. Stir and take off the heat.
Pour the spices into the tomato/yogurt mixture. Add the salt and mix carefully.
Serve only one or two spoonfuls per person to accompany meal.

🔷 If you turned to the *Food Combining* section, you would find tomatoes and yogurt listed as incompatible. This recipe is a good example of how the right combination of spices and herbs can help to balance incompatible foods.

Pitta can add extra cilantro, cumin seeds and curry leaves, avoid the cayenne, chili and hing, and eat this in moderation.

Pickles and Chutneys

All pickles and chutneys will add color, sparkle and taste to a meal. But their main role in the Ayurvedic cuisine is to stimulate agni, raise the digestive fire and help with the digestive process. Like raitas, pickles and chutneys are eaten in small quantities.

Carrot Pickle

2   carrots (about 1 cup)
3   tablespoons oil
1   teaspoon black mustard seeds
1   pinch hing
1   teaspoon pickle masala powder
2   pinches salt

Wash and thoroughly dry the carrots. Peel and chop very fine.

Heat the oil in a small pan on medium heat and add the mustard seeds and hing. Stir until the seeds pop. Cool and pour over the carrots.

Add the pickle masala powder and salt. Stir well.

Cover and store in refrigerator. Keeps for up to 1 month AS LONG AS not a drop of water gets into the pickle, such as using a wet spoon to get the pickle out of the jar. The water will cause fermentation and the pickle will spoil.

Eat in very small quantities with meal.

Pickle masala powder can be purchased at Indian grocery stores. It is not the same as the masala powder recipe given in this book.

Pitta and vata should eat this sparingly.

Turmeric Pickle

1   cup fresh turmeric roots
3   tablespoons oil
1   teaspoon black mustard seeds
1   pinch hing
1   teaspoon pickle masala powder
2   pinches salt

Wash and thoroughly dry the turmeric roots. Peel and chop very fine.
Heat the oil and add the mustard seeds and hing. Stir until the seeds pop. Cool and pour over the chopped turmeric.
Add the pickle masala powder and salt. Stir well.
Cover and store in refrigerator. Keeps for up to 1 month AS LONG AS not a drop of water gets into the pickle, such as using a wet spoon to get the pickle out of the jar. The water will cause fermentation and the pickle will spoil.
Eat in very small quantities with the meal.

▨ Turmeric root and pickle masala powder are available from most Indian grocery stores. Turmeric root looks a little like a small ginger root but is brilliant orange under the skin.

Pitta should use less hing and mustard seed.

Green Mango Pickle

1 large unripe mango
3 tablespoons oil
1 teaspoon black mustard seeds
1 pinch hing
1 teaspoon pickle masala powder
2 pinches salt

Wash and thoroughly dry the mango. Cut off the ends, slice and carefully remove the large seed. Do not peel the mango. Now chop the pulp and peel quite finely.

Heat the oil and add the mustard seeds and hing. Stir until the seeds pop. Cool and pour over the chopped mango.

Add the pickle masala powder and salt. Stir well.

Cover and store in refrigerator. Keeps for up to 1 month AS LONG AS not a drop of water gets into the pickle, such as using a wet spoon to get the pickle out of the jar. The water will cause fermentation and the pickle will spoil.

Eat in very small quantities with meal.

▨ Pickle masala powder is available from Indian grocery stores

Pitta can decrease the amount of hing and mustard seed.

Cilantro Chutney

Makes approximately 2 cups

3   cups fresh cilantro
1   cup water
1   cup unsweetened, shredded coconut
½   small green chili, chopped
1   inch piece of fresh ginger, peeled and chopped fine
1   tablespoon ghee
½   teaspoon cumin seeds
½   teaspoon black mustard seeds
1   pinch hing
4   curry leaves, fresh or dried
½   fresh lime
¼   teaspoon salt

Wash the cilantro leaves and remove the stems. Put it in a blender along with the water, coconut, chili and ginger.

Blend at high speed until well mixed and a finely ground paste. It may be necessary to stir it down several times.

Heat a saucepan on medium and add the ghee, cumin seeds, mustard seeds, hing and curry leaves. Cook until the seeds pop. Cool and mix well into the cilantro paste.

Squeeze in the juice of the lime, add the salt and stir gently.

Eat a dab with each bite of food.

Store in the refrigerator. Good for 2-3 days.

This recipe is balancing for tridosha. Pitta might want to decrease the chili, salt and mustard seeds even though the cilantro is very cooling.

Coconut Chutney

V↓ P↓ K↓

Makes approximately 3 cups

2   cups unsweetened, shredded coconut
1½ inch piece of fresh ginger, peeled and chopped fine
½   small green chili, chopped
1   tablespoon fresh cilantro leaves
2   cups water
2   tablespoons ghee
½   teaspoon black mustard seeds
½   teaspoon cumin seeds
1   pinch hing
4   curry leaves, fresh or dried
½   fresh lime
¼   teaspoon salt

Put the coconut in a blender with the ginger, green chili and cilantro. Add the water and blend until smooth.

Heat a saucepan on medium and add the ghee, mustard seeds, cumin seeds, hing and curry leaves. Cook until the seeds pop.

Pour the spices into the blended mixture. Squeeze in juice from the lime, stir in salt and gently mix.

Store in refrigerator. Keeps for 2-3 days.

This is tridoshic, but kapha can increase the hing, mustard seeds and chilies.

Mint Chutney

Makes approximately 2 cups

3	cups fresh mint leaves
1	cup water
1	cup shredded, unsweetened coconut
½	small green chili, chopped
1	inch piece of fresh ginger, peeled and chopped fine
1	tablespoon ghee
½	teaspoon cumin seeds
½	black mustard seeds
1	pinch hing
4	curry leaves, fresh or dried
½	lime
¼	teaspoon salt

Wash the mint leaves and discard long stems.

Put the mint, water, coconut, chili and ginger into a blender and blend on medium until it is a well mixed and finely ground paste.

Heat a saucepan on medium and add the ghee, cumin seeds, mustard, hing and curry leaves. Cook until the seeds pop. Cool and add to the mint paste. Squeeze in the juice from the lime. Add the salt and stir well.

Store in refrigerator. keeps for 2-3 days.

The mint helps make this calming for pitta, but it is still best to leave out the chili.

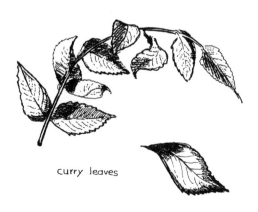

curry leaves

Peanut Chutney

V↓ P↑ K↓

1   cup roasted and ground peanuts
1   teaspoon cayenne
¼   teaspoon salt

Blend the peanuts, cayenne and salt until well mixed and use 1 teaspoon per meal on the side of the plate.

Pitta should use a very light touch with the cayenne.

Sesame Seed Chutney

V↓ P↓ K↓

1   cup roasted and ground sesame seeds
1   teaspoon cayenne
¼   teaspoon salt

Blend sesame seeds, cayenne and salt until well mixed and use 1 teaspoon per meal on the side of the plate.

Less cayenne for pitta.

Tomato Chutney

Makes 1 cup

1	good-sized tomato, chopped fine
½	large onion, chopped fine
2	tablespoons safflower oil
1	teaspoon cumin seeds
1	teaspoon black mustard seeds
1	pinch hing
1	pinch salt
3	curry leaves, fresh or dried
1	tablespoon cilantro leaves, chopped
¼	teaspoon turmeric
½	small green chili, chopped <u>or</u> 1 pinch cayenne
1	teaspoon Sucanat or other sugar

Heat a frying pan on medium heat and add the oil, cumin and mustard seeds. When the seeds pop, add the hing, salt, curry leaves, cilantro, turmeric, chili and onions. Sauté until the onions are translucent.

Put in the tomatoes and sugar. Stir gently to coat them well.

Cover and turn off the heat. Let sit for a few minutes and serve.

NOTE: Do not make this in a copper pot or store it in a metal container other than stainless steel, because the acid in the tomatoes will interact with the metal and ruin the chutney.

▨ Pitta should use less hing, mustard seed and chili.

Breads

In Ayurvedic cooking, most breads are flat breads rather than ones made with yeast. They are usually cooked on the top of the stove—baked, fried or deep-fried. The bread should be made fresh before each meal if possible, to have the maximum amount of prana. Bread is often used in place of a "spoon" for eating the meal.

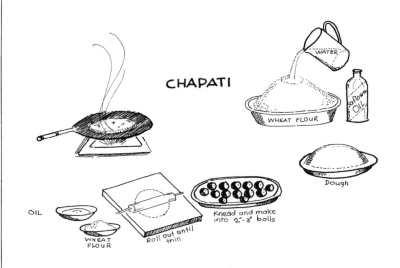

CHAPATI

WATER

safflower OIL

WHEAT FLOUR

Dough

OIL

WHEAT FLOUR

Roll out until thin

Knead and make into 2"-3" balls

Chapatis

Makes approximately 1 dozen

4 cups Laxmi brand (or whole wheat) flour
2 cups water
¾ teaspoon salt
  small bowl of safflower oil

Mix the flour and the salt.
Make a well in the center of the flour and begin to add the water, about ¼ cup at a time. Knead thoroughly with your hands after each addition.
Keep adding water until you have a stiff dough that will not stick to your hands. You may need to use more or less water than the recipe calls for, depending upon the humidity of the climate.
Cover the dough and set it aside for half an hour.
Now take a small handful of dough, about the size of a small egg, and roll it into a ball.
Roll the ball in flour and flatten a little with your palms or a rolling pin.
Brush or pat one side with oil, without putting it on the edges.
Lightly dip the oiled side into flour. Fold over in half, covering the oiled side, and fold in half again. Pinch the edges together.
Dip both sides in flour and roll out until thin and even. To roll it into a nice round shape, it helps to give the chapati a bit of a turn each time before you roll it again.
Place the chapati on a hot, seasoned—but not oily—chapati or frying pan until it bubbles up and the bottom has brown spots.
Dab with oil and flip it over, cooking it until lightly brown on bottom.
The chapati should be cooked in 2-4 minutes.
Wrap them in a clean tea towel until ready to serve.

Laxmi is Indian whole wheat flour and has a grainy texture. It can be purchased at Indian grocery stores. You may use whole wheat pastry flour in place of chapati flour.

Tridosha balancing.

Plain Puri

Makes approximately 1 dozen

4   cups Laxmi brand (or whole wheat) flour
2   cups water (approximately)
¾   teaspoon salt
     oil for deep frying

Put the flour and salt in a shallow bowl. Mix well.

Make a well or dent in the center of the flour and start adding the water, about ¼ cup at a time, kneading well with your hands after each addition. The dough will be stiff, forming a nice smooth ball that is not sticky.

Cover and let sit for ½ an hour.

Heat oil for frying until a drop of dough comes instantly to the surface.

Break off a small handful of dough, about a 1½ - 2 inch ball. Oil a board lightly and roll out the ball into a circle of 4 - 5 inches, about ⅛-inch thick. Repeat until you use all the dough.

Deep fry each puri separately, until golden brown and puffed, turning over and over frequently.

Remove them with a slotted spoon and place on a paper towel to drain. Serve hot.

 Balancing for tridosha, but kapha must eat in moderation.

Spicy Puri

Makes approximately 1 dozen

4	cups Laxmi brand (or whole wheat) flour
½	teaspoon ajwan seeds
½	teaspoon cumin seeds
½	teaspoon sesame seeds
¾	teaspoon turmeric
2	pinches cayenne
2	tablespoons fresh cilantro, chopped finely
¼	teaspoon salt
2	cups water, approximately
	oil for deep frying

Put the flour in a shallow bowl and add all other ingredients except for the water. Mix well.

Make a well or dent in the center of the flour and start adding the water, about ¼ cup at a time, kneading well with your hands after each addition. The dough will be stiff, forming a nice smooth ball that is not sticky.

Cover and let sit for ½ an hour.

Heat oil for frying until a drop of dough comes instantly to the surface.

Break off small handfuls of dough, enough to roll into 1½-2 inch balls. Oil a board lightly and roll out the balls into circles of 4-5 inches, about ⅛-inch thick. Deep fry each puri separately, until golden brown and puffed, turning over and over frequently.

Remove them with a slotted spoon and place on a paper towel to drain. Serve hot.

▨ Pitta should reduce or leave out the cayenne.

Sweets

Desserts and other sweets are usually served with the main meal, rather than at the end. Ayurvedic tradition says that sweets eaten at the end of the meal may cause congestion and sinus problems. Sweets are also served at religious celebrations.

Indian puddings or khirs tend to be very liquid. They are often spiced with saffron and cardamom, for these spices help neutralize the mucous-forming properties of milk, as well as give the pudding a delicious taste. Sometimes the khir will have charoli nuts—a small tasty, Indian nut. If you don't have access to charoli nuts, the closest substitutes are pistachio nuts and almonds. In India, these sweets would be made with granulated jaggery, which is a natural, unprocessed sugar from sugar cane juice. If you can't get jaggery, good substitutes are Turbinado and Sucanat sugar, both made from natural sugar cane juice.

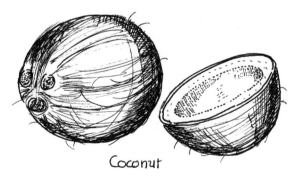

Coconut

Almond Khir

Serves 4

40 whole almonds, soaked overnight and peeled
5 cups of milk
¼ teaspoon cardamom
1 rounded teaspoon charoli nuts (optional)
1 pinch saffron
1 cup Sucanat or other sugar (or to taste)
1 tablespoon ghee

Soak the saffron in 1 tablespoon warm water for 10 minutes.
Put the almonds in a blender with 1 cup of the milk and blend until liquefied. Bring the remaining 4 cups of milk to a boil and add the cardamom, charoli nuts, soaked saffron and blended almonds. Stir in the sugar and ghee. Cook for 5 minutes at a gentle boil, stirring occasionally. Serve warm.

Kapha needs to add a pinch of dry ginger and eat this in moderation.

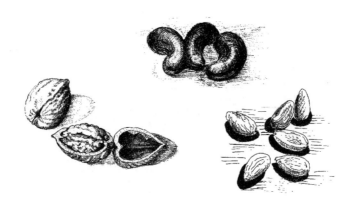

Creamed Wheat Khir

Serves 4

1	cup creamed wheat
½	cup *ghee*
8	cups milk
1	heaping tablespoon sliced almonds
1	tablespoon charole nuts (optional)
1	cup Sucanat or other sugar (or to taste)
½	teaspoon ground cardamom

Heat a large pot and add the *ghee*. Stir in the creamed wheat and keep stirring until it is light brown in color and fragrant.

Pour in the milk, stirring briskly, to prevent lumps forming. Then mix in the nuts, cardamom and sugar.

Bring to a boil and stir as it thickens, to keep it from sticking. Cook and stir for another 2 minutes. Cover and turn off the heat.

Balances all *doshas*, but *kapha* must eat only occasionally.

Carrot Khir

Serves 8 to 10

1   pinch saffron
1   tablespoon milk
½   cup ghee
2   cups carrots, peeled and finely grated
8   cups milk
1   heaping teaspoon charoli nuts (optional)
½   teaspoon cardamom
1   cup Sucanat or other sugar (or to taste)

Soak the saffron in 1 tablespoon of milk for 10 minutes.
Meanwhile, heat a pot on low heat and add the ghee.
Stir in the carrots and keep stirring until they are light brown and fragrant, about 5 minutes.
Pour in the milk, then add the charoli nuts, cardamom, soaked saffron and sugar. Stir a few times and bring to a boil.
Continue to stir as it thickens, to keep it from sticking.
Cook and stir for 5 minutes on a low boil. Cook longer if you want it a little thicker.
Can be served either warm or cool.

You can cut the quantities in half.

🔷 Kapha can eat this occasionally, especially if it is made with goat's milk. Charoli nuts can be purchased at Indian grocery stores.

Cornmeal Khir

Serves 6

1   pinch saffron
1   tablespoon milk
½   cup ghee
1   cup cornmeal
8   cups milk
1   heaping tablespoon sliced, skinned almonds
¼   teaspoon ground cardamom
1   tablespoon charoli nuts (optional)
1   cup Sucanat or other sugar (or to taste)

Soak the saffron in 1 tablespoon of milk until soft and yellow, about 10 minutes. Heat a pan over a medium flame and add the ghee. Stir in the cornmeal and keep stirring until it is light brown and fragrant.

Mix the milk and soaked saffron into the cornmeal, stirring briskly to prevent lumps forming. Then add the almonds, charoli nuts, cardamom and sugar.

Bring to a boil while stirring frequently to keep it from sticking.

Cook and stir for 2 minutes after it boils. Serve warm.

▨ Tridosha balancing, but best eaten in moderation, especially by kapha. The cardamom and saffron help with digestion.

Date Khir

Serves 4

1   pinch saffron
1   tablespoon milk
1   cup dried, pitted dates
5   cups milk
¼   teaspoon cardamom
1   rounded teaspoon charoli nuts (optional)
1   tablespoon ghee
½   cup Sucanat or other sugar (or to taste)

Soak the saffron in 1 tablespoon of milk for 10 minutes.
Put the dates and 1 cup of the milk into the blender and blend until liquefied.
Bring to a low boil the remaining 4 cups of milk and add the cardamom, charoli nuts, soaked saffron and blended dates. Stir in the sugar and ghee.
Continue cooking for 5 minutes at a gentle boil, stirring occasionally to keep from sticking.
Serve warm.

Kapha can add a pinch of ginger and eat in moderation.

Fruit is not normally eaten with dairy products, but the dried dates do not have the same souring effect as fresh ones. The saffron and cardamom also help with the digestion.

Poppy Seed Khir

Serves 4

1   pinch saffron
1   tablespoon milk
¼   cup white poppy seeds
4   cups milk
¼   teaspoon cardamom
1   pinch nutmeg
1   heaping teaspoon charoli nuts (optional)
1   tablespoon ghee
½   cup Sucanat or other sugar (or to taste)

Soak the saffron in 1 tablespoon milk for 10 minutes.
Dry roast the poppy seeds in a heavy pan or skillet on top of the stove, stirring constantly until the seeds are golden brown and popping.
Put the seeds and 1 cup of the milk into a blender and blend until liquefied.
Bring to a low boil the remaining 3 cups of milk and add the cardamom, nutmeg, charoli nuts, soaked saffron and blended poppy seeds. Stir in the sugar and the ghee.
Continue to cook at a gentle boil for another 5 minutes, stirring occasionally. Serve warm.

 Kapha can eat this in moderation,

Medicinal Uses: This khir is excellent for inducing sleep and for alleviating diarrhea.

Rice Khir

V↓ P↓ K↓

Serves 4

1	pinch saffron
1	tablespoon milk
½	cup ghee
½	cup creamed rice
8	cups milk
1	heaping tablespoon sliced almonds
1	tablespoon charoli nuts (optional)
¼	teaspoon cardamom
1	cup Sucanat or other sugar (or to taste)

Soak the saffron in 1 tablespoon milk for 10 minutes.

Heat a medium-sized pot and add the ghee. Stir in the creamed rice and keep stirring until it is light brown and fragrant.

Pour in the milk and soaked saffron, then add the almonds, charoli nuts, cardamom and sugar.

Bring to a boil and keep stirring to prevent lumps forming. Cook and stir as it thickens for 2-3 minutes. Turn off the heat and cover until ready to serve.

Kapha should eat this only very occasionally.

Roasted Vermicelli Khir

Serves 4

1 pinch saffron
1 tablespoon milk
1 cup roasted vermicelli
3 tablespoons *ghee*
6 cups milk
1 cup Sucanat or other sugar (or to taste)
2 teaspoons charoli nuts (optional)
¼ teaspoon cardamom, ground
1 tablespoon almonds, peeled and sliced

Soak the saffron in 1 tablespoon of milk for 10 minutes.
Break the vermicelli into small pieces.
Heat a saucepan and add the ghee and vermicelli. Stir and mix well for 1 minute.
Pour in the milk, sugar, cardamom, charoli nuts, almonds and soaked saffron. Stir and bring to a gentle boil.
Cook until the vermicelli is soft, about 10 minutes.

Roasted vermicelli is available from Indian grocery stores. If unavailable, regular vermicelli can be used by sautéing it an extra minute or two in the ghee.

Kapha should add a good pinch of ginger and eat this only occasionally.

Sweet Potato Khir

Serves 4

1   pinch saffron
1   tablespoon milk
½   cup ghee
2   cups sweet potatoes, grated
8   cups milk
1   heaping teaspoon charoli nuts (optional)
¼   teaspoon cardamom
1   cup Sucanat or other sugar (or to taste)

Soak the saffron in 1 tablespoon of milk for 10 minutes.

Peel and wash the sweet potatoes, then grate very finely.

Heat a large pot and add the ghee. Stir in the grated sweet potatoes and keep stirring them until they are light brown and fragrant.

Pour the milk over the sweet potatoes slowly, stirring well. Add the charoli nuts, cardamom, soaked saffron and sugar. Stir a few times and bring to a boil. Keep stirring as the khir thickens to keep it from sticking.

Cook for about 5 minutes at a gentle boil. Turn off the heat and cover until ready to serve.

A pinch or two of dry ginger will help make this acceptable as an occasional treat for kapha.

Tapioca Khir

Serves 5

1 cup tapioca
5 cups water
1 pinch ground cardamom
1 pinch nutmeg
1 teaspoon charoli nuts (optional)
1 pinch ginger
1 cup milk, warmed
½ cup Sucanat or other sugar (or to taste)

Wash the tapioca two times, drain and set aside for 1 hour.
Then boil the water and add the tapioca, stirring constantly.
Mix in the cardamom, nutmeg, charoli nuts and ginger.
Cook, uncovered, on medium low heat until the tapioca is soft, approximately 10 minutes.
Remove from the heat, stir in the warm milk and sugar. Cover.
Best served warm.

 Easy to digest and especially good after an illness.

Creamed Wheat Squares

Makes approximately 3 dozen

4 tablespoons ghee
1 cup creamed wheat
2 cups hot water
1 tablespoon charoli nuts or finely chopped almonds
5 tablespoons Sucanat or other sugar (or to taste)
¼ teaspoon ground cardamom
   shredded coconut

Heat a saucepan on medium heat and add the ghee. Put in the creamed wheat and stir it constantly until it is fragrant and slightly brown.
Add the water, cover and simmer for 5 minutes.
Turn off the heat and stir in the nuts, sugar and cardamom.
Grease a large flat pan or cookie sheet with ghee. Put the creamed wheat mixture on the pan and slowly pat it flat with your hands until it is about ¼ inch thick. Lightly sprinkle the top with coconut.
With the tip of a sharp knife, cut into bite-sized diamond shapes.

▨ An extra pinch or two of ginger will help make this suitable for occasional use by kapha.

Carrot Halva

Serves 6

1 pinch saffron
1 tablespoon water
2 cups carrots, finely grated
6 tablespoons ghee
1 cup milk
⅓ cup Sucanat or other sugar (or to taste)
½ teaspoon ground cardamom
1 tablespoon sliced almonds <u>or</u> 1 rounded teaspoon charoli nuts

Soak the saffron in 1 tablespoon of water for at least 10 minutes.
Melt the ghee in a heavy pot over a low heat and add the carrots. Cook and stir for 5 minutes or so, until the carrots smell fragrant and are slightly brown. Add the milk, stirring constantly, and the soaked saffron and other ingredients. Cook over low heat, uncovered, until all the liquid is absorbed, about 12-15 minutes. Stir frequently to keep from sticking.
Serve in small dishes as a dessert, about ¼ cup per person.

Charoli nuts come from India and there is no close "western" equivalent to them. They can be purchased at Indian grocery stores.

This recipe is balancing for all doshas but kapha should eat in moderation and make it with goat's milk, if possible.

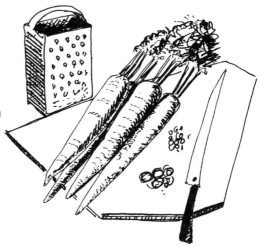

GAJAR Carrot

Shankhar Pali

Serves about 20 to 30

1 cup milk
1 cup ghee
1 cup Sucanat or other sugar
6 cups unbleached, all-purpose flour (approximately)
  oil for deep frying

In a saucepan, mix the milk, sugar and ghee. Heat on low just until the sugar is melted.

Put the flour in a wide bowl. Make a well in the center. Slowly add the heated liquid, about ¼ cup at a time, to the flour. Mix well with your hands, until you have a stiff, smooth dough that is not sticky.

Cover the dough and set it aside for ½ an hour or so.

Take about ¼ of the dough, form into a ball and roll it out with a rolling pin until barely ¼ inch thick. Cut into ½ inch squares with a sharp knife.

Heat oil for deep frying until a bit of dough sizzles instantly to the top when you drop it in. Make sure the oil doesn't smoke.

Put the squares in the oil until the surface is covered and slowly fry them to a lovely golden brown, turning them frequently.

Drain well and serve as a snack with chai or for celebrations.

These will keep well in a covered container for up to a month.

Recipe can be cut in half for a smaller group.

◈ Good to add a little ginger for kapha and only eat occasionally.

Sheera

Serves 4 to 5

½ cup ghee
2 cups creamed wheat
4 cups hot water
1 cup Sucanat or other sugar (or to taste)
1 tablespoon charoli nuts <u>or</u> sliced almonds <u>or</u> pistachio nuts
1 pinch ground cardamom

Heat a pot and add the ghee.
Add the creamed wheat and cook on medium heat, stirring constantly, until light brown with a fragrant smell.
Turn off the heat and add the hot water, stirring briskly.
Cook and stir on medium heat until it begins to thicken.
Cover and turn down the heat to low and cook for 1 minute.
Stir in the sugar, nuts and cardamom until well mixed. Serve warm.

Add a pinch or two of ginger for kapha and eat in moderation.

Shrikhanda

Serves 4

1   pinch saffron
1   tablespoon milk
4   cups yogurt
2   teaspoons charoli nuts (optional)
¼   teaspoon ground cardamom
⅛   teaspoon nutmeg
1   cup Sucanat or other sugar (or to taste)

Soak the saffron in 1 tablespoon of milk for 10 minutes.
Put the yogurt in a bowl and add the charoli nuts, cardamom, nutmeg, soaked saffron and sugar. Mix together well and serve fresh.
Keeps 2-3 days in the refrigerator.

Kapha should only eat this occasionally, with a pinch of ginger.

Beverages

Ayurveda recommends that you have a warm drink with your meal to help with digestion, but that the quantity should be no more than a cup. Ideally, after a meal, the stomach contains one-third solid food, one-third liquid and one-third empty. At the end of a meal, a cup of lassi—made with diluted yogurt or buttermilk—can be a good aid to digestion. The tasty Indian tea or Chai sometimes is taken with a meal or between meals. Drinks and herbal teas are also used for their medicinal value. Ayurveda does not recommend ice cold drinks at any time, because the cold is shocking to the system and can kill the digestive fire.

Rose

Fresh Cilantro

CUMIN FENNEL CORIANDER

Pachak Lassi

Serves 4

2 cups water
½ cup plain yogurt
1 inch piece of fresh ginger
½ teaspoon cumin seeds or powder
⅛ teaspoon salt
1 tablespoon cilantro leaves, chopped

Put all ingredients, except cilantro, into a blender and blend for 1-2 minutes until liquid. Garnish with cilantro.

◈ Balancing for all doshas. The blending kindles the agni principle in the yogurt, making this combination excellent for digestion when taken at the end of a meal.

Spicy Lassi

Serves 4

2 cups water
½ cup of plain yogurt
2 tablespoons Sucanat or other sugar (or to taste)
½ teaspoon fresh, grated ginger <u>or</u> ¼ tsp. dry ginger
½ teaspoon ground cardamom

Put all ingredients into a blender and blend for 1-2 minutes. Adjust sugar according to taste and dosha.

Good for all doshas, especially kapha. Blending the yogurt kindles the agni principle.

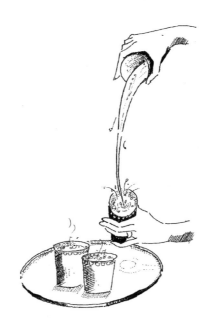

Sweet Lassi

Serves 4

2   cups water
½   cup plain yogurt
2   tablespoons Sucanat or other sugar
1   drop rosewater

Put all ingredients into a blender and blend for 1-2 minutes. Adjust sugar according to dosha.

Tridoshic but especially balancing for pitta. Blending of the yogurt helps kindle the agni principle.

Sidha Dugdham *(Medicated milks)*

For Kapha Disorders

No. 1
½ teaspoon peppercorns, ground
1 cup milk
¼ cup water

Mix all ingredients and heat to boiling point. Continue to cook on medium heat, stirring constantly, until there is 1 cup of liquid left.

▨ This is good as a liver and gallbladder flush. It is used effectively for a high-kapha person with lymphatic congestion.

No. 2
½ teaspoon pippali, ground
1 cup milk
¼ cup water

Mix all ingredients and heat to boiling point. Continue to cook on medium heat, stirring constantly, until there is 1 cup of liquid left.

▨ This is good for chronic bronchial congestion, kapha-type asthmatic congestion and is also effective in kapha-type respiratory tract allergies.

No. 3
½ teaspoon turmeric
1 cup milk
¼ cup water

Mix all ingredients and heat to boiling point. Continue to cook on medium heat, stirring constantly, until there is 1 cup of liquid left.

▨ This is good for pharyngitis, laryngitis and hoarseness of the voice. It is also effective for acute tonsillar congestion and acute kapha-pitta conditions of the lungs. It is a natural antiseptic.

recipes continue ➤

No. 4

½ teaspoon powdered ginger
1 cup milk
¼ cup water

Mix all ingredients and heat to boiling. Continue to cook on medium heat, stirring constantly, until there is I cup of liquid left.

▧ This is good for mucus in the colon, chronic indigestion and kapha-vata respiratory conditions like dry cough and emphysema.

For Vata and Pitta Disorders

¼ teaspoon ground cardamom
¼ teaspoon ground charoli nuts (optional)
¼ teaspoon ground almonds
1 cup milk
¼ cup water

Mix the nuts and spice together. Add this mixture to the milk and water. Heat to the boiling point. Continue to cook on medium heat, stirring constantly, until there is 1 cup of liquid remaining.

▧ This is a generalized tonic and energizer. It is also effective in chronic fatigue syndrome and in conditions of sexual debility or low libido.

Breakfast Tea

½   teaspoon fresh ginger, grated
½   teaspoon cinnamon
1   pinch cardamom
1   cup water

Boil the water and add the spices. Cover, turn off the heat and let sit a few minutes.

Good for all doshas. Pitta might want to add ¼ cup of milk.

Lunch Tea

V↓ P↓ K↓

⅓   teaspoon cumin seeds
⅓   teaspoon coriander seeds
⅓   teaspoon fennel seeds
1   cup water

Boil the water and add the spices. Turn off the heat and cover. Let stand for 5 minutes. Strain and sweeten according to your constitution.

Dinner Tea

V↓ P↓ K↓

⅛   teaspoon fennel seed
⅓   teaspoon cinnamon
⅓   teaspoon chamomile
1   cup water

Boil the water and add the spices. Turn off the heat, cover and let sit for a few minutes. Sweeten according to constitution.

Chai

Serves 4

3	cups water
4	cloves
2	pinches ground nutmeg
2	pinches ground cinnamon
2	pinches ground cardamom
½	inch piece of fresh ginger
1	teaspoon black tea (or dandelion root or lemon grass)
1	cup milk
2	teaspoons sweetener of your choice

Boil the water with the spices for 2 minutes.
Add the tea and simmer for two minutes.
Add the milk and heat until hot but not boiling.
Add sweetener and serve.

You may vary the amounts of the milk and sugar according to taste and dosha. Of course, increasing the milk and/or sugar can provoke kapha.
If you use caffeinated tea, the cardamom will help neutralize the effects of the caffeine.

Fresh Ginger

Mint Chai

Serves 4

½ teaspoon fresh ginger, chopped fine
3 pinches powdered ginger
3 pinches ground cardamom
1 stick cinnamon
2 pinches nutmeg powder
1 teaspoon coriander seeds
1 teaspoon cumin seeds
½ cup fresh mint leaves <u>or</u> 1 tablespoon dried mint
3-4 whole cloves
3 cups water
1 cup milk

Boil the water and add the tea, spices and milk. Simmer for a few minutes.
Strain and serve.

Tea for *Vata* Constitution

Serves 1

¼   teaspoon fresh ginger, grated
¼   teaspoon ground cardamom
¼   teaspoon cinnamon
¼   teaspoon ajwan
1   cup water

Boil the water and add the spices. Turn off the heat and let sit for a few minutes. Sweeten according to taste.

🔲 Especially calming and grounding for vata.

Tea for *Pitta* Constitution

V↓ P↓ K↓

Serves 1

¼   teaspoon cumin
¼   teaspoon coriander
¼   teaspoon fennel
¼   teaspoon rose petals
¼   teaspoon fresh cilantro
1   cup water

Boil the water and add the spices. Turn off the heat and cover. Let stand for 5 minutes. Strain and sweeten according to your constitution.

🔲 Stimulates digestion. Also very calming for pitta.

Tea for *Kapha* Constitution

Serves 1

¼   teaspoon dry ginger
⅓   teaspoon ground cloves
¼   teaspoon dill seed
¼   teaspoon fenugreek seed
1   cup water

Boil the water and add the spices. Cover, turn off the heat and let sit a few minutes.

Especially calming for kapha.

Tea Masala

1   teaspoon powdered ginger
½   teaspoon ground cloves
½   teaspoon black pepper
½   teaspoon ground cardamom
¼   teaspoon nutmeg powder
¼   teaspoon cinnamon

Mix the spices together and use 1 pinch per cup of water when making tea.

Tridoshic, but pitta can go easy on the black pepper and cloves.

Agni Tea

V↓ P↓ K↓

Serves 6 to 8

1 quart water
⅛ teaspoon cayenne pepper
½ handful minced ginger root
2 tablespoons Sucanat or other sweetener
⅛ to ½ teaspoon rock salt

Bring all of the ingredients to a boil.
Boil for 20 minutes.
Take the pot off the burner, cool for a few minutes and then add the juice of
½ lime. *Do _not_ boil the lime juice.*
You can pour this into a thermos and drink it throughout the day.

This tea kindles agni and is good to drink just before a meal. It may be a little heating for pitta, so they can leave out the cayenne if necessary.

Extras

In this section there are several useful recipes, including one for ghee.

Ghee (Clarified Butter)

1   pound unsalted butter

Put the butter in a heavy, medium-sized pan. Turn on the heat to medium until butter melts.

Turn down the heat until the butter just boils and continue to cook at this heat. Do not cover the pot. The butter will foam and sputter for awhile and then begin to quiet down. Stir it occasionally.

In 12-15 minutes, it will begin to smell like popcorn and turn a lovely golden color. Whitish curds will begin to form on the bottom of the pot. When these whitish curds turn a light tan color, the ghee (butter) is ready. Take it off the heat immediately, for the ghee is most likely to burn at this stage—and it burns quickly! Burned ghee has a nutty smell and a dull, slightly brownish color. The cooking time should not be longer than 15 to 20 minutes, depending on the kind of pan and the heat source.

Let the ghee cool until just warm. Skim off and save any foam left on the top, for it has medicinal qualities. It is good on hot rice. Pour the ghee through a fine sieve or layers of cheesecloth into a glass container with a tight lid. Discard the curds at the bottom of the saucepan.

Ghee can be kept on the kitchen shelf, covered. It does not need refrigeration. The medicinal properties are said to improve with age. Don't ladle out the ghee with a wet spoon or allow any water to get into the container, as this will create conditions for bacteria to grow and spoil the ghee.

Once you become familiar with the cooking process, you can make 2 or 3 pounds of butter into ghee at a time.

Ghee is a digestive. It helps to improve absorption and assimilation. It nourishes ojas, tejas and prana. It is good for improving memory and lubricates the connective tissue. Ghee makes the body flexible and, in small doses, is tridoshic. Ghee is a *yogavahi*—a catalytic agent that carries the medicinal properties of herbs into the seven *dhatus* or tissues of the body. Ghee pacifies pitta and vata and is acceptable, in moderation, for kapha. Persons who already have high cholesterol or suffer from obesity should be cautious in using ghee. Ghee is not to be used when there are high ama (toxic) conditions.

Two pounds of butter will fill a quart jar with ghee.

Masala Seasoning

1   teaspoon ground cloves
1   teaspoon ground cardamom
1   teaspoon ground black pepper
5   bay leaves
1   teaspoon cinnamon
5   teaspoons cayenne (more or less according to taste)

Grind all ingredients together in a mortar and pestle or blender until well mixed and finely ground.
Store covered.

▨ The amount of cayenne in the recipe does not take into consideration the number of heat units of the peppers used. This can vary widely but, if you purchased cayenne, it will be fairly hot.

After-Dinner Seeds for Digestion

½   cup fennel seeds
¼   cup toasted coriander seeds
¼   cup sesame seeds
1   tablespoon cumin seeds
1   tablespoon ajwan seeds
2   pinches salt (preferably black or sea)
1   tablespoon hot water

Pick over the fennel seeds for any twigs or tiny stones.
Dissolve the salt in 1 tablespoon of water.
Heat a heavy cast iron frying pan on medium heat. Put in the fennel seeds and roast, stirring constantly, until slightly brown, about 2 minutes. Sprinkle on the salt water and stir and toast until dry and fragrant. Pour into a dish.
Roast the remaining seeds, each kind separately, for a minute or so, until fragrant and slightly brown. Add to the dish of fennel and mix well.
Store in a glass jar.

Eat a teaspoonful after lunch and supper for good digestion and sweet breath.

▩ These coriander seeds have the hard outer shell removed and are often roasted with turmeric. They are available from Indian grocery stores.

Chapter 8

FOODS FOR HEALING

NOTE: Just a reminder that these are suggestions only, and not meant to substitute in any way for the advice of a qualified physician. Sometimes you will find a variety of suggestions and approaches for the same condition, such as the common cold or gas. Because Ayurvedic teachings consider each person to be unique, a specific approach may be just the one that brings you some relief, so enjoy finding out what suits your needs.

You will find here a variety of terms used to describe the effect a food or herb may have on each of the three doshas, such as promote, provoke, stimulate, etc. These terms all mean that the dosha will be temporarily upset. If intake of this particular food continues, the dosha will become aggravated and begin to manifest disease.

There are a few Ayurvedic herbs mentioned here that may not be familiar to most people. For information and sources for these, write or call The Ayurvedic Institute.

FRUITS

Apples   come in many colors and varieties, but for Ayurvedic healing we shall look at their ripe/sweet quality and their sour quality. When sweet, apples are slightly astringent, cooling and the vipaka (post-digestive effect) is sweet. On the other hand, sour apples are mainly astringent in taste, cooling and the vipaka is pungent. Apples are good for pitta and kapha; but too drying for vata unless they are well-cooked and spiced. The skin of the apple is hard to digest and can cause gas. Do not eat the seeds of the apple, for they are astringent and bitter and can cause vata aggravation.

1. Raw apple, even though it stimulates vata, relieves constipation, bleed-

ing gums and over-salivation. It is traditionally used for stomatitis—an inflammation of the oral mucous membrane or cold sores in the mouth. One can peel and chew an apple thoroughly, an hour or so after a meal, to help regularize the bowels and to clean the tongue and teeth. The skin can be peeled off easily if the apple is soaked in hot water for 15 minutes.

2. Apple juice is helpful for burning sensations in pitta conditions such as gastritis, colitis and bladder infections.

3. To help stop diarrhea and dysentery, peel and cook a couple of apples until soft. Add a pinch of nutmeg, saffron and 1 teaspoon of ghee and eat slowly.

4. For a delicious dessert, remove the skins and the core from 5 apples. Blend or mash the mixture to make a pulp. Add honey to taste and mix thoroughly. Add ⅛ teaspoon of powdered cardamom, a pinch each of saffron and nutmeg and 10 drops of rose water or a few organic rose petals. About ½ cup of this "honey-apple pulp" can be eaten at least an hour after the meal. Ayurveda says do not take milk, yogurt or fish at least 4 hours either before or after eating this pulp, because it makes a bad food combination.

This dessert is a good energetic food for the heart muscles, relaxes the blood vessels and helps to relieve swelling of the feet. Traditionally it is used as a food for people with varicose veins, insomnia, sexual debility and arthritis.

Bananas Unripe bananas are astringent and cooling with a pungent vipaka. They increase vata and decrease pitta and kapha. Ripe bananas are sweet and heating with a sour vipaka. They decrease vata and increase pitta and kapha. Bananas are aphrodisiac and energize muscle, fat, nerve and reproductive tissues.

PRECAUTIONS:

Do not take any liquids until at least an hour after eating a banana.

Do not eat bananas at night.

Do not eat bananas with milk.

Do not eat bananas with yogurt.

Do not eat bananas when there is fever, edema, vomiting or cough with mucus and runny nose.

(Use ripe bananas here unless otherwise stated.)
1. For emotional, obsessive eating habits, 1 banana chopped up with 1 teaspoon of ghee and a pinch of cardamom is very effective. This is also useful for hypoglycemia, constipation or muscle cramps.
2. If there is burning urination due to insomnia, constipation and acidic pH, eating 1 or 2 bananas with a pinch of cumin powder helps. This should be taken in between meals.
3. In cases of dry cough or cough without much mucus and accompanied by chest pain, eat 1 or 2 bananas with 1 teaspoon of honey and 2 pinches of ground black pepper, 2 or 3 times a day.
4. Two bananas, 5 fresh figs and 5 fresh dates chopped together with a spoonful or two of honey, plus 2 pinches of ginger powder, is a whole meal and a good tonic for muscular weakness or muscle wasting.
5. In cases of chronic bronchial asthma, insert about 7 cloves into a peeled banana and keep it overnight. Next morning eat the banana and the cloves. One hour later, drink 1 cup of hot water with 1 teaspoon of honey. This will give energy to the lungs and the wheezing should be reduced.
6. In cases of diarrhea, try eating 2 green, chopped bananas with 1 teaspoon of ghee and 2 pinches of ginger powder. Drink 1 cup of hot water an hour later.
7. For excess urination often associated with diabetes, try eating 1 unripe banana with ⅓ cup of bitter melon juice, once a day.
8. To stop hiccoughs, eat 2 chopped bananas mixed with 1 teaspoon of *ghee*, ½ teaspoon of honey and 2 pinches of ginger powder.

Cherries are sweet, sour, astringent and heating with a pungent vipaka. They pacify vata and kapha but may provoke pitta when taken in excess.
1. Cherries are good for mental fatigue, stress and insomnia. Eating 10 to 20 cherries daily may help in these conditions.
2. For premenstrual syndrome and/or for excess menstrual flow, with vata and kapha symptoms such as aches, water retention or white discharge, eat about 10 cherries on an empty stomach daily, for a week before the onset of menstruation.
3. When a long car drive causes motion sickness and/or headache, eat 7 cherries. It helps.
4. For poor vision, redness and/or prominent blood vessels in the eyes and/or on the tip of nose, eat about 15 cher-

the eyes and/or on the tip of nose, eat about 15 cherries daily on an empty stomach.

5. If your skin is very dry, apply a pulp of cherries as a mask at night before bed. Leave on for 15 minutes. This will give you a beautiful complexion.

6. A pulp made from powdered cherry seeds can help in cases of eczema and psoriasis. Spread on skin and leave for 10-15 minutes.

Coconut is sweet and cooling with a sweet *vipaka*. The flesh of the coconut is hard, heavy and oily, and the center is liquid. Because of the hard shell, coconut falls into the nut category. Coconut pacifies *vata* and *pitta,* but may aggravate *kapha* in excess. Coconut oil is useful for external application.

NOTE: Coconut water is the juice inside the coconut; coconut milk is made from grating the white flesh and mixing it with a cup or so of water. Let sit a few minutes and squeeze out the coconut milk.

1. For itchy eczema, apply burned, powdered coconut meat to the skin.
2. For burning skin or sunburn, apply coconut oil.
3. For burning urination, try drinking 1 cup of coconut water.
4. For measles, chicken pox or other rash, coconut water will help.
5. If hair is thinning and/or falling out, apply coconut oil to the scalp.
6. In cases of dandruff, itching scalp or vitiligo (patches of skin without pigment), apply coconut milk locally.
7. Try using coconut oil for fungal infections of the nails.
8. For profuse menstrual bleeding, taking 1 cup of coconut water with ½ teaspoon of rock candy powder (or organic sugar) may help.
9. For cases of ulcers from colitis, an enema with 1 pint of coconut milk can bring some relief.
10. A tooth powder made from finely ground coconut shell with a pinch of edible camphor is beneficial for receding and bleeding gums.

Dates (Fresh) are sweet and cooling with a sweet *vipaka*. They decrease *vata, pitta* and *kapha,* but should be used in moderation by *kapha*. Dates generally promote health. They are energizing and nourishing. Date sugar is a healthy substitute for white sugar.

1. Mix 5 fresh, chopped dates, 1 teaspoon of *ghee* and 2 pinches of black pepper. Eat this mixture in the early morning around 5:30 to 6:00 AM.

the power of the intestines to absorb and assimilate foodstuff. It will bind the stool, improve muscle tone and nourish the bones.

2. A poultice of date sugar is effective in healing a painful muscle.
3. Date sugar is a good source of iron.
4. Soak 10 fresh dates in a quart jar of ghee. Add 1 teaspoon of ginger, ⅛ teaspoon of cardamom and a pinch of saffron. Cover loosely. Keep this in a closed warm place for 1 week. Then eat 1 date daily in the early morning. This will help anemia, sexual debility and chronic fatigue syndrome.
5. The above formula (#4) is good during pregnancy for morning sickness and anemia.
6. For palpitations and chest pain, 2 dates mixed with 2 teaspoons of honey is good.
7. For teething children, give them dried dates to chew on.
8. For diarrhea during teething, give the child ½ teaspoon date sugar mixed with 1 teaspoon honey, 2 or 3 times a day.
9. Date drink: Soak 5 fresh dates in a glass of water overnight. Next day liquefy this mixture in the blender and drink. This will give you energy and vitality.

Figs *(Fresh)* are sweet and cooling, with a sweet vipaka and are heavy to digest. They calm vata and pitta, and promote kapha.
They are a good source of iron and build up the blood.
Figs are excellent for children.
Individuals with low agni should not eat figs at all.
People suffering from diarrhea and dysentery should avoid figs.
Do not eat figs with milk. It may cause diarrhea and indigestion.

1. For strengthening the gums, teeth and tongue, try eating 4 figs and chewing them properly, once a day.
2. In cases of chronic indigestion, heartburn and diarrhea, try eating 7 fresh figs and do not drink any water for at least 1 hour afterward. Consider fasting on figs for 3 days and it may heal the condition.
3. For constipation in children, give 3 figs soaked in warm water.

4. For burning urination, eating 4 fresh figs daily, an hour after meals, may help.
5. In cases of asthma, eat figs with a pinch of pippali first thing in the morning to get some relief.
6. In cases of debility, weakness, dry cough and evening rise of temperature, one can eat 2 figs with a mixture of 1 teaspoon of honey and 1 teaspoon of ground licorice root in the early morning. Do not eat or drink for at least 2 hours afterward.
7. For sexual debility in women and men, eat daily, after breakfast, 3 figs with 1 teaspoon of honey. One hour later take a glass of lassi. Also gently rub warm castor oil on the lower abdomen at bedtime for 1 month. This will help restore sexual energy.

Grapes Green grapes are sour, sweet and heating with a sweet vipaka. They stimulate kapha and pitta, and are acceptable for vata only in moderation. Red, purple or black grapes are tridoshic. They are sweet, sour and astringent, with cooling energy and a sweet vipaka. They are a gentle laxative and are rich in iron, hence are good for iron-deficient anemia.

1. Mix 1 cup of grape juice with 1 teaspoon of fresh onion juice and 1 teaspoon of honey. If one takes this mixture once a day for 45 days, an hour before bed, it will help increase the sperm count and endurance. Kapha individuals should add a pinch of trikatu—made from equal parts of dry ginger, black pepper and pippali.
2. An individual having repeated attacks of cystitis, urethritis or burning urination should try 1 cup of grape juice with a pinch of rock salt and 1 teaspoon of cumin powder. Take this 2 or 3 times a day.
3. For chest pain, pleurisy and muscle weakness, try 1 cup of grape juice, 1 teaspoon of honey and ½ teaspoon of ginger powder on an empty stomach twice a day.
4. For excess pitta conditions causing anger, hate and a burning sensation in the stomach or urethra, drink a mixture of 1 cup of grape juice, ½ teaspoon of cumin, ½ teaspoon of fennel and ½ teaspoon of sandalwood powder.
5. For fever, use the same mixture as in #4.
6. For sexual debility, mix 1 cup of grape juice, a pinch of pippali, ½ teaspoon of rock candy or natural sugar and ½ teaspoon of ashwagandha. Drink 1 hour before bed.

7. One ounce of finely ground powder of dry grape seeds and a pinch of edible camphor is a useful mixture for brushing the teeth. It helps gingivitis, pyorrhea and receding gums.

8. For chronic cough, asthma and respiratory allergies, try the following: mix 1 part seedless grapes, 1 part ghee and ½ part honey. Put it in a jar or crock with a cork or a loose lid. Keep it in a warm place covered by a blanket for 15 days. Strain. Take 1 teaspoon twice a day.

9. Eating a handful of raisins every day, an hour after meals, can help with conditions of anemia, enlarged liver or spleen and constipation.

Lemons   are sour and heating and have a sour vipaka. They are sharp, digestive and laxative and stimulate salivation and digestive juices in the stomach. They calm down vata, detoxify balanced pitta but may stimulate aggravated pitta and kapha doshas. In Ayurvedic literature, lemons have a great healing value.

Never take lemons with milk, mango, tomatoes or when one has a peptic ulcer.

1. In cases of nausea, vomiting and/or indigestion, make a mixture of 1 part lemon juice and 1 part honey. Dip your index finger into this mixture and lick it slowly.

2. For indigestion and to eliminate gas, a mixture of 1 cup of cool water, 1 teaspoon of lemon juice and ½ teaspoon of baking soda may be helpful. Stir this mixture and drink it quickly, as it produces carbon dioxide, which aids these conditions.

3. For morning sickness in pregnant women or nausea in children, take a sip, every fifteen minutes, of a mixture of 1 cup of coconut water and 1 teaspoon of lemon juice to calm the stomach.

4. For kidney stones and gravel in the urine, a mixture of 1 cup of water, 1 teaspoon each of lemon juice and cilantro juice may be very helpful. Take this 2 or 3 times a day.

Limes   are sour, slightly bitter and cooling but their vipaka is sweet. Lime calms vata and is all right in moderation for pitta. However the sour property can aggravate pitta if taken in excess. Lime stimulates kapha and can cause excess salivation. Lime is useful with hot, spicy foods to cool down their pitta provoking nature. Lime stimulates the secretion of digestive enzymes and is useful for indigestion. It can be an effective antidote to alcohol. Lime should not be used when one has a cold, congestion and/or cough.

1. To improve the appetite, chew some lime with a pinch of rock salt.
2. Lime pickle, about 1 teaspoon, used with the main meal, improves digestion and absorption of minerals, as well as the taste of the food.
3. For acute indigestion, squeeze the juice from ¼ of a lime in 1 cup of warm water. Add ½ teaspoon of baking soda and drink quickly.
4. For acid indigestion, take the juice of ¼ of a lime, mixed with 1 cup warm water and 1 teaspoon of rock candy or organic sugar.
5. For heartburn, nausea or hyperacidity, take ½ lime and hold it on a fork or stick over a flame. Put ¼ teaspoon of sugar and a pinch of baking soda on the lime. Let the fire penetrate the skin, charring it a little. Cool and chew this up, skin and all. This is also helpful for headache, for motion sickness and morning sickness.
6. A mixture of 1 glass of heated, then cooled, water and 1 teaspoon of lime juice, if taken, sip by sip, every fifteen minutes for the whole day, will help to relieve a burning sensation of the urethra.
7. For individuals with high blood pressure who need diuretic action without sodium and potassium loss, a mixture of 1 cup coconut juice, 2 teaspoons of lime juice and 1 cup of cucumber juice may be beneficial.
8. A glass of hot water with 1 teaspoon each of honey and lime juice may be a useful drink to take in the morning for conditions of obesity and high cholesterol.

Mango: Green, Unripe is sour, astringent and cooling with a pungent vipaka. They disturb all three doshas. Generally, green mangos are used for making special Indian chutney and pickles. When prepared in this way, mangos are not aggravating. They help digestion and improve the flavor of food.

Never drink water right after eating green mango. It may cause bronchitis, cold, cough and respiratory congestion. Wait at least an hour.

Do not eat a large quantity of unripe mango. It may cause rash, nausea, diarrhea and indigestion or heartburn.

1. Boil grated, green mango with 4 parts of water for 3 to 5 minutes. Add jaggery or another organic sugar to taste and 1 teaspoon of lime juice.

Strain the mixture. This is a wonderful drink called *pahne* that helps to nourish the plasma. It is also very good for people suffering from dehydration.

2. Peeled green mango skin can be dried in the sunlight and used in the same way as curry leaves for lentil soups. It helps the digestion of lentils. The skins will last for a year.

3. For burning eyes, put the pulp of grated green mango on the eyelids at bedtime.

4. To help sunstroke, eat a few pieces of green mango with a pinch of salt. Wait at least an hour before drinking any liquids.

Mango: Yellow, Ripe is sweet and heating, with a sweet vipaka. In moderation, it balances the tridoshas. It acts as an energizer and an aphrodisiac. Patients of diabetes should consult with their physician before eating ripe mangos.

1. Eating 1 ripe mango daily and, an hour or so later, drinking 1 cup of warm milk with 1 teaspoon of ghee is good for energy and vitality.

2. Mango is good for pregnant women and it helps lactation.

3. Eating a chapati daily with 1 cup of mango juice gives energy, joy and contentment.

4. For intestinal worms, 1 teaspoon of roasted, powdered mango seed 2 or 3 times a day with 1 teaspoon of honey is quite beneficial.

5. For diarrhea, take 1 teaspoon of roasted, powdered mango seed, with a small cup of yogurt, twice a day, during the day.

6. To help stop a nosebleed, use 3 to 5 drops of fresh mango seed juice in each nostril. Grate the fresh mango seed, then put it in a cheese cloth and squeeze out the juice.

7. For dandruff, mix ½ teaspoon powdered mango seed, ½ teaspoon haritaki powder and ⅓ cup of milk. Apply on the scalp at night and wash it out the next morning.

8. Drinking 1 cup fresh, ripe mango juice, followed an hour or so later by ½ cup of milk with a pinch of cardamom, pinch of nutmeg and 1 teaspoon of ghee, gives energy, vitality and acts as an aphrodisiac. It helps relieve constipation, diarrhea and is good for the patient of high blood pressure or heart conditions.

9. If some pitta individuals are sensitive to mango, they should try the previous recipe (#8). If this does not agree with them, then they should avoid mangos.

Melons are sweet and cooling with a sweet *vipaka*. They are watery, unctuous and heavy to digest. They calm *vata* and *pitta,* and may provoke *kapha*. Most melons have similar actions. They tend to have a diuretic action and to be an aphrodisiac.

1. To alleviate burning sensations associated with excess *pitta*, eat melon.
2. For some relief from rashes, eat melon and rub the rind over the skin.
3. To help control acne, rub the inner skin of melon rind on the skin at bedtime and leave on overnight. This application also makes the skin soft.
4. For burning urination, cystitis and urethritis, try eating melon with a pinch of coriander powder sprinkled on it.
5. Eat melon, chewing it slowly, to help bleeding gums.

Oranges are sour, sweet and heating with a pungent *vipaka*. They pacify *vata*. Sweet oranges are acceptable for *pitta* in moderation but sour ones provoke *pitta*. Taken in excess, oranges stimulate *kapha*.

1. One cup of fresh orange juice with a pinch of rock salt is good for fatigue after exercise. Add 10 drops fresh lime juice to calm *pitta*.
2. One cup of orange juice, with ½ teaspoon of natural sugar and a pinch of cumin, is good for bleeding gums, hemorrhoids and bloodshot eyes.
3. For alcoholic or any other drug-induced hangover, 1 cup of orange juice with 1 teaspoon of lime juice and pinch of cumin powder can be useful.
4. For individuals with burning urination, edema and high blood pressure, a mixture of 1 cup of orange juice and ½ cup of coconut juice may be beneficial 2 or 3 times a day.
5. In cases of anxiety and increased heart rate, 1 cup of orange juice with 1 teaspoon of honey and a pinch of nutmeg powder can be effective.
6. Sweet orange juice can be a nourishing drink during the entire period of pregnancy.
7. For indigestion and gas, 1 cup of orange juice with a pinch of ajwan and hing is a good digestant and helps to relieve gas.

Papayas are sweet, heating and have a sweet *vipaka*. They calm down *vata* and are okay in moderation for kapha. *Pitta* must use them only about once a week. Papayas are generally helpful for cough, asthma, liver and spleen dysfunctions. They help control worms. Papayas have enzymes that help with digestion. The juice is a blood thinner and can help to prevent heart attacks.

Papayas contain natural estrogen. They should not be taken during pregnancy.

1. For indigestion, acute gastritis and hyperacidity, try drinking 1 cup of papaya juice with 1 teaspoon of organic sugar and 2 pinches of cardamom.
2. For an enlarged spleen, 1 cup of papaya juice, followed by ½ cup of warm milk with a pinch of ginger powder can help. Take this on an empty stomach twice a day.
3. Rubbing the inner skin of papaya over areas of the skin affected by eczema and dermatitis can bring some relief.

Peaches are sour, sweet, and astringent with a heating energy and a sweet *vipaka*. They pacify *vata* and may promote *pitta*. Eating one peach may calm *kapha*, but more than one may stimulate mucous secretions in the lungs. Due to their heating energy and pungent *vipaka*, unripe peaches will help to kill any worms in the colon.

1. For worms, eat 1 or 2 green peaches on an empty stomach in the early morning. After ½ hour, drink 2 teaspoons of castor oil mixed with 1 cup of hot ginger tea. This helps to eliminate worms and their ova from the colon. Do not eat or drink anything for at least 3 hours after this.
2. In cases of kidney or bladder stones, drink 1 cup of peach juice mixed with ½ teaspoon of coriander powder on an empty stomach, twice a day. Do not eat tomatoes, spinach, salt or tamarind with these conditions.
3. In cases of high fever with burning urination due to high *pitta*, take 1 cup of peach juice with ½ teaspoon of cumin powder and 1 teaspoon of rock candy powder or natural sugar.
4. Eating 1 peach an hour after meals helps relieve constipation.
5. When there are symptoms of *vata* aggravation such as dry tongue, pal-

pitation, fatigue and exhausted voice, drink 1 cup of peach juice with a pinch of rock salt, 10 drops of lime juice and 1 teaspoon of rock candy powder or natural sugar. One can drink this mixture 3 to 4 times a day for relief.

6. For sweating hands and feet, eat 1 peach daily an hour after each meal.
7. The patient with high blood pressure can try taking 1 cup of peach juice with a pinch of cardamom powder and 1 teaspoon of coriander powder, 2 or 3 times a day.
8. For bedwetting in children, give them 1 cup of peach juice with 1 teaspoon of vidanga powder, once a day for a few days. If vidanga is unavailable, substitute a pinch of ground black poppy seeds.

Pears are sweet, astringent and cooling with a pungent vipaka. Due to their cooling property, they slightly stimulate vata, calm down pitta and, owing to their diuretic and pungent actions, they help to reduce kapha.
Do not eat pears if you have a dry cough, diabetes, arthritis or sciatica.
Never eat pears with rice, yogurt, milk or melons.

1. Eat a pear by itself to help stop diarrhea.
2. For poor appetite, abdominal discomfort and excess thirst, eating pears will help.
3. Pears are good for bleeding and inflamed gums.
4. Eating 2 pears in the morning will help flush the liver and help to pass small gallstones and kidney stones. But do not eat or drink anything for at least for 2 hours after eating them.
5. For urinary tract inflammation, eat 2 pears on an empty stomach.

Pineapples are sweet, sour and heating with a sweet vipaka. It soothes vata and is okay for kapha, but only small amounts of the ripe fruit are suitable for pitta. Ripe pineapple has a nice fragrance. Pineapple juice by itself is not good for a pitta constitution and pitta disorders, and it should not be given to children under seven. Unripe pineapple is heavy to digest. It may cause fullness of the stomach, lack of taste and heaviness of the tongue, so eat it with caution. Never eat pineapple in the early morning on an empty stomach. It will upset the stomach and cause acidity.

Never eat dairy or drink milk within two to three hours before or after eating pineapples.

Pregnant women should never eat unripe pineapple, as it may induce a miscarriage.

1. About an hour and a half before a meal, one can sip a glass of pineapple juice with a pinch of black pepper and a pinch of salt. It stimulates digestive enzymes and promotes hunger. Pineapple juice taken this way is especially helpful if you will be having meat for a meal.
2. Pineapple juice helps to relieve constipation.
3. In cases of indigestion, nausea or diarrhea, one can observe a fast and drink 1 cup of sweet pineapple juice with a pinch of ginger, black pepper and ½ teaspoon of organic sugar. Take this 3 times a day.
4. In cases of abdominal distention, try drinking 1 cup of pineapple juice with a pinch of ajwan.
5. For intestinal worms, try eating 4 pieces of pineapple, with a pinch of black pepper and rock salt, an hour after a meal. This will help dissolve worms, yeast and amoeba.
6. The external application of warm, pineapple pulp on the site of piles can relieve hemorrhoids.
7. In cases of severe itching from eczema, rub fresh pineapple juice at the site of the lesion to stop the itching.
8. For burning urination, 1 glass of pineapple juice, with ½ teaspoon of natural sugar or dextrose, helps.
9. In cases of nicotine toxicity due to heavy smoking, one can chew small pieces of pineapple with ½ teaspoon of honey to help reduce smoking habits.

Pomegranates are sweet, sour, astringent and cooling with a sweet vipaka. They increase vata, and decrease pitta and kapha. They promote the production of red blood cells and are good for anemia, fever and heart conditions.

Do not drink pomegranate juice with meat, milk or yogurt.

1. For children with a cough, try giving them a drink of ½ cup of pomegranate juice, with a pinch of ginger powder and a pinch of pippali powder.

2. For nausea and vomiting, a mixture of ⅓ cup pomegranate juice, 1 teaspoon rock candy powder or natural sugar and ½ teaspoon grated fresh ginger once or twice a day will often work.
3. When there is blood and mucus in the stools, drink ½ cup pomegranate juice with a pinch of clove powder and 2 pinches of ginger powder, 2 or 3 times a day.
4. Two drops of fresh pomegranate juice in each nostril will help to stop a nosebleed.
5. For rash, hives and hot flashes, try drinking 1 cup of pomegranate juice, with 1 teaspoon of rock candy powder or organic sugar and 5 to 10 drops of lime juice, 2 or 3 times per day.
6. For morning sickness, take a sip of pomegranate juice that has been mixed with 1 teaspoon of rock candy or organic sugar.
7. In the case of dehydration, 1 cup of pomegranate juice mixed with ½ cup of grape juice, 1 teaspoon of rock candy powder (or organic sugar) and a pinch of ginger powder will help.
8. For burning eyes, put 1 drop of pomegranate juice in each eye at night.

Raspberries are sweet, slightly sour and astringent and cooling with a pungent vipaka. They stimulate vata and calm kapha dosha. Pitta can eat them occasionally.
Never eat more than two handfuls of raspberries at a time, because it may cause vomiting.
Do not eat milk, yogurt or cheese with raspberries as it may cause hemorrhoids, ulcers and skin diseases.

1. For burning urination, eat about 20 raspberries with 1 teaspoon rock candy powder or natural sugar sprinkled over them and then drink 1 cup of water. This may help to stop the burning sensation and inflammation of the urinary tract.
2. In cases of bleeding gums, hemorrhoids or profuse menstruation, try chewing about 10 to 20 raspberries, 2 or 3 times a day, on an empty stomach.
3. In any bleeding disorder, drink 1 cup of raspberry juice with a pinch each of ground cumin and ground fennel to help slow down the bleeding.

Strawberries are sour, sweet, astringent and heating and have a pungent vipaka. In moderation, they are suitable for tridosha, but overeating strawberries can disturb all three doshas and may affect the lungs and stomach, leading to coughing and vomiting.

Do not mix strawberries with other food, especially milk, yogurt or honey. Eat them alone or leave them alone.

1. Eating 10 strawberries daily may help the patient of pulmonary tuberculosis or anemia.

Watermelon is sweet and cooling, with a sweet vipaka. It is heavy and diuretic. It provokes kapha and vata, and relieves pitta. It binds the stools and flushes the kidneys.

Never eat watermelon within three hours after food. Do not eat it at night or on a cloudy, rainy day for it may cause edema or abdominal pain. Never eat it with any grains because it will affect digestion adversely.

Due to its cooling and heavy qualities, watermelon in excess can cause respiratory congestion.

Watermelon increases intraocular pressure, hence is not good for anyone suffering from glaucoma.

Too much watermelon can inhibit semen.

1. One cup of watermelon juice with a pinch of cumin powder, drunk 3 times a day on an empty stomach, is traditionally used in urethritis, cystitis and in the case of scanty, burning urination.

2. One can drink 1 cup of watermelon juice with ¼ teaspoon of coriander powder in cases of kidney pain. This will give the kidneys a good flushing and help to remove small stones and crystals. Use this 2 to 3 times a day.

3. Grind ½ cup of fresh watermelon seeds to make a fine pulp. Add 1 teaspoon of natural sugar and ½ teaspoon of ghee and eat it on an empty stomach. This helps to strengthen weak muscles.

4. In cases of skin rash, eczema and skin allergic conditions, eat the red part of watermelon and rub the white part of the rind on the skin. This can give some relief to the itching and burning.

5. An unusual recipe for beautiful skin: Take a medium-sized watermelon and make a round hole at one end, saving the piece you cut out. Insert into the hole 2 teaspoons of uncooked basmati rice, 1 teaspoon of tur-

meric powder, 1 teaspoon of sandalwood powder, ¼ teaspoon of edible camphor, a pinch of saffron and 1 teaspoon of lime juice. Close the hole by putting the cut piece of skin back in place. Keep the watermelon in a warm, dry place for a week. After a week, cut open the watermelon and collect the inner pulp. Dry it in a hot, dry place, but not in direct sun. This soft, powdered pulp is used for cosmetic purposes. If one applies this powder daily to the face, the skin will look young and beautiful. It helps remove wrinkles, acne, eczema and other skin conditions.

6. Drinking 1 cup of watermelon juice with 1 teaspoon of honey, in the early morning on an empty stomach, helps to reduce edema in congestive heart conditions.

VEGETABLES

Bitter Melon is bitter and cooling with a pungent vipaka. It can provoke vata, while its bitter quality can soothe pitta and kapha. It is a good food for fever, anemia, diabetes and worms.

Note: Bitter melon is an Indian vegetable available from specialty stores and Indian groceries.

1. During fever, take 2 tablespoons of fresh bitter melon juice 3 times a day, to bring down the temperature.

2. Cooked bitter melon, as in *Bitter Melon Bhaji*, is good for cleansing the liver and can help in anemia.

3. For intestinal worms and parasites, try 1 tablespoon of bitter melon juice with a pinch of trikatu, 3 times a day, ½ hour before each meal. Do this for 1 week and the worms should vanish.

4. Cooked bitter melon is laxative and can be used to relieve constipation and hemorrhoids.

5. Insulin-dependent diabetics can help to regulate the insulin dose by taking 2 tablespoons of bitter melon juice with ¼ teaspoon of turmeric powder, 15 minutes before each meal.

6. Jaundice, hyperthyroidism and migraine headaches can all be helped by putting 5 drops of fresh bitter melon juice in each nostril in the morning and again in the evening.

Carrots are heating with a pungent vipaka, so they pacify kapha and stimulate pitta if eaten in excess. Raw carrots are rough and have astringent rasa, so they disturb vata. Cooked carrots are sweet, pacifying vata. Carrots are digestive and laxative, and can detoxify the body.

1. For anemia, mix ½ cup each of fresh carrot and fresh beet juice with a pinch of cumin powder. Take this twice a day on an empty stomach.
2. Take 1 cup of carrot juice mixed with 2 teaspoons of cilantro juice twice a day on an empty stomach to give relief for hemorrhoids.
3. For chronic sprue—a disease endemic to tropical regions—take 1 cup carrot juice with a pinch of trikatu 2 times a day.
4. Chronic indigestion can be helped by a glass of carrot juice with 1 pinch of ginger powder.
5. Thoroughly mix ½ cup each of carrot juice and aloe vera juice. Take this twice a day as part of an anticancer program.

Cilantro, sometimes called Chinese parsley or coriander leaf, is sweet, astringent and cooling with a sweet vipaka. It balances all doshas and is especially good for kindling gastric fire, for nausea, fever, cough and quenching thirst.

1. When the skin has been burned, use fresh cilantro juice to soothe it. Take the juice internally 3 times a day, 2 teaspoons at a time, and put some of the pulp directly on the skin.
2. For fever, take 2 teaspoons cilantro juice 3 times a day to help lower the temperature.
3. For burning urination, try mixing ½ cup rice water—made from cooking ¼ cup of rice in 2 to 3 cups of water—with 2 teaspoons of cilantro juice. Take this 3 times a day.
4. To get relief from coughing, mix together 2 teaspoons cilantro juice, 1 teaspoon of jaggery or another organic sugar and ½ teaspoon ginger. Take 1 teaspoon as needed.
5. For conjunctivitis, apply the pulp of fresh cilantro leaves on the eyelids.

Garlic has all tastes except salty, is heating with a pungent vipaka. It calms vata and kapha, and provokes pitta. Garlic is a good tonic for heart, lungs and muscles, and helps to prevent gas and breathlessness. It can be used as a painkiller and as an aphrodisiac.

1. For earache, try using garlic oil. Make this by boiling 1 teaspoon of sesame oil with about ¼ clove of garlic. It is best to try this in a metal

spoon with a long handle. Strain, cool to body temperature and put 3 drops in the ear at bedtime.

2. To relieve an enlarged spleen and splenic pain, mix ½ teaspoon each of garlic powder and haritaki and ¼ teaspoon pippali. Take with warm water at night. Or try 1 chopped garlic clove, a pinch of pippali, 2 pinches of haritaki and 1 tablespoon of aloe vera juice. Take this 2 or 3 times a day.

3. For chronic indigestion, take a mixture of ¼ teaspoon garlic powder, ½ teaspoon trikatu and a pinch of rock salt before lunch and supper. Or try 1 clove of garlic, chopped with ¼ teaspoon cumin powder, a pinch each of rock salt and trikatu and 1 teaspoon of lime juice before meals.

4. Garlic is a good food for obesity, arthritis, high cholesterol and chronic cough. Use 1 clove garlic chopped fine, ½ teaspoon grated ginger root and ½ teaspoon lime juice before each meal.

5. For chronic cough, make a mixture of 4 parts garlic powder to 1 part trikatu and enough honey to mix it together. Take this twice a day.

6. Take 108 cloves of garlic, peel them and string them on a yellow thread long enough to go over the head, making a necklace or mala. Put them around your children's necks and they will never catch any flus, coughs or colds!

7. For acute abdominal pain, try 10 drops of garlic oil with ½ teaspoon of ghee.

8. Garlic milk: Mix together 1 cup of milk, ¼ cup water and 1 clove garlic, chopped. Boil this gently until 1 cup of liquid remains. Drink this at bedtime. It promotes sound sleep and also helps arthritis. It has some aphrodisiac qualities as well.

Onions are pungent and heating. If raw, they have a pungent vipaka, while cooked onions are sweet with a sweet vipaka. Raw onions are aggravating to vata and pitta, and soothing to kapha. When cooked, they calm vata and kapha, but still can aggravate pitta when taken in quantity.

1. For convulsions and fainting, cut an onion and inhale the aroma until the tears come.

2. In the case of acute epileptic convulsion, squeeze 2 drops of fresh onion juice in each eye. This will help to stop the convulsion.

3. For hemorrhoids, mix 1 tablespoon of onion juice, 1 teaspoon of rock candy or organic sugar and ½ teaspoon of ghee. Take internally twice a day.

4. To lower a high fever, wrap grated onion pulp in a wet piece of cloth

and apply to the forehead and then the navel (belly button), for about 10 minutes at each location.

5. When there is sexual debility, take 1 tablespoon of onion juice mixed with 1 teaspoon of fresh ginger juice, 2 times a day.
6. For rapid heartbeat, take 2 teaspoons of onion juice mixed with ½ teaspoon sitopaladi, 2 times a day.
7. To help with conditions of high cholesterol, take 1 teaspoon of onion juice mixed with a pinch of trikatu, before lunch and supper.

Radishes *(especially daikon—the long, white radish)* are pungent and heating with a pungent vipaka. They pacify kapha but pitta types should use them only occasionally. Raw radish aggravates vata but cooked radish is okay for vata in moderation. Radishes can help to relieve gas, flush the liver and get rid of intestinal worms.

1. Fresh radish juice, 2 teaspoons with a pinch of ginger, is good for kindling agni and improving digestion.
2. For gas and distention caused by gas, try taking 2 teaspoons of radish juice with 2 pinches of ajwan and a pinch of hing. Do this twice a day on an empty stomach.
3. When there is liver dysfunction, 2 teaspoons of radish juice with a pinch of coriander powder may relieve the pain.
4. For intestinal worms, try 2 teaspoons of radish juice with ½ teaspoon of vidanga, 2 or 3 times a day.

Spinach Raw spinach is astringent, slightly pungent and sweet, cooling, and has a pungent vipaka. Cooked spinach is astringent, sour, heating, and has sweet vipaka. It is laxative and can be heavy to digest. Spinach should not be eaten by anyone with gallstones or kidney stones.

1. Spinach juice can be applied externally to the skin when there is swelling.
2. The symptoms of bronchial asthma can be relieved by taking ⅓ cup spinach juice and a pinch of pippali, twice a day.
3. For a chronic cough, try ½ cup of spinach soup and ¼ teaspoon ginger, twice a day on an empty stomach.

Tomatoes belong to the nightshade family and can be green, yellow or red. The green and yellow ones are sour, sweet and heating with a pungent vipaka. They provoke all three doshas.

Red tomatoes are also sour and sweet with a pungent vipaka. They have a cooling effect in the stomach and a heating influence in the intestines. Red tomatoes provoke all doshas when they are raw. Although Ayurveda says tomatoes are generally quite toxic to the system, they are okay once in a while if cooked with spices such as cumin, turmeric, and mustard seeds.

Tomatoes are not good for acidity, arthritis, sciatica, kidney and gallstones. The seeds of raw tomatoes may cause abdominal pain.

1. Because meat is heavy to digest, 1 hour after eating it, try drinking 1 cup of tomato juice with a pinch of cumin powder to help with the digestion.
2. For indigestion, 1 cup of tomato juice, ¼ teaspoon of black pepper, a pinch each of hing and rock salt mixed together may bring relief.
3. For mental fatigue and insomnia, try 1 cup of tomato juice, with 2 teaspoons of organic sugar and 2 pinches of nutmeg, between 4 and 5 in the afternoon. Have dinner between 6 and 7 p.m., and that evening you should get a sound sleep.
4. To reduce fat and body weight in obesity, take 1 cup of tomato juice with 2 pinches of trikatu in the early morning. Wait 2 hours before eating or drinking anything else.
5. Where there is dry cough, breathlessness and chest pain, take 1 cup of tomato juice with 1 teaspoon of turmeric, 2 teaspoons of organic sugar and a pinch of ground clove. Take this on an empty stomach and don't eat or drink for at least an hour.

HOUSEHOLD HERBS

Ajwan is pungent and heating with a pungent vipaka. It calms vata and kapha, and may stimulate pitta. It is an excellent painkiller and heart tonic. It also helps get rid of gas in the intestine. It is hot, sharp and penetrating, hence good for kindling agni and digestion.

1. For acute abdominal pain with indigestion, try chewing ½ teaspoon of ajwan with a pinch of salt, then drinking 1 cup of warm water.
2. For nausea and vomiting, try chewing ½ teaspoon ajwan with 1 clove, 2 or 3 times a day, followed by ½ cup of warm water.
3. For productive cough and *kapha*-type cold and fever, ½ teaspoon of ajwan, ¼ teaspoon pippali and ½ teaspoon poppy seeds steeped in 1 cup of hot water for 10 minutes may help. Drink this twice a day.

4. For acute throat irritation and coughing, chew ½ teaspoon of ajwan and drink 1 cup of warm water.

5. For dry cough, try chewing ¼ teaspoon ajwan mixed with 1 teaspoon organic sugar.

6. For excess urination, chew a mixture of ½ teaspoon ajwan and ½ teaspoon of black sesame seeds. Follow this with ½ cup warm water.

7. A mixture of ¼ teaspoon ajwan and ½ teaspoon vidanga can help get rid of intestinal worms. Take 3 times a day after meals, for 2 weeks.

Bay Leaf is sweet, pungent and heating with a pungent vipaka. It increases pitta and decreases vata and kapha. It promotes sweating, is a digestant and stimulant, kindles gastric fire and can be a diuretic.

1. For indigestion, try ½ teaspoon ground bay leaf steeped in 1 cup of hot water for 10 minutes. Add a pinch of cardamom and drink it after food.

2. For abdominal pain, ¼ teaspoon ground bay leaf, ¼ teaspoon ajwan and 1 teaspoon of honey, 2 times a day before lunch and dinner can help.

3. For intestinal worms, ½ teaspoon bay leaf, ½ teaspoon vidanga and 1 teaspoon of honey before lunch and dinner for 15 days should get rid of them.

4. When there is the threat of miscarriage, ¼ teaspoon of ground bay leaf and ½ cup of milk can be boiled together, cooled and drunk twice a day to help protect the fetus.

5. To help regulate blood sugar in diabetics, try ½ teaspoon of ground bay leaf, ½ teaspoon turmeric and 1 tablespoon of aloe vera gel. Take this 2 times a day before lunch and dinner, until the blood sugar returns to normal.

6. For cough and asthma, ½ teaspoon bay leaf powder, ¼ teaspoon pippali and 1 teaspoon of honey, 2 or 3 times a day will help.

Black Pepper is pungent and heating, with a pungent vipaka. It decreases vata and kapha, and increases pitta. It is useful for digestion, cough, worms and promoting health to the lungs and heart.

1. For hoarseness of voice, try ¼ teaspoon of black pepper powder and 1 teaspoon of ghee. Eat this slowly, after lunch and dinner.

2. For cough, try ¼ teaspoon of black pepper powder and 1 teaspoon of honey after food.
3. For chronic fever, make a tea of 1 teaspoon of holy basil (*tulsi*) and 1 cup of hot water. Add ¼ teaspoon of black pepper powder and 1 teaspoon of honey. Take this 2 or 3 times a day.
4. Diarrhea can be helped with 1 cup of lassi and 2 pinches of black pepper powder, stirred together and taken twice a day.
5. For lower abdominal pain, try a mixture of a pinch each of black pepper and hing and 1 teaspoon of *ghee*.
6. For an allergic rash, mix 1 teaspoon of *ghee* and a pinch of black pepper. Take this orally as well as applying it to the affected area.

Cardamom is sweet, pungent and heating with a sweet vipaka. It decreases vata and kapha, and increases pitta. It is good for cough, breathlessness, burning urination and hemorrhoids. It is a digestant and improves the flavor of food.

1. For sexual debility, drink 1 cup of hot milk with ½ teaspoon of ghee and a pinch each of cardamom and hing.
2. For bleeding disorders, a pinch each of cardamom, saffron and nutmeg, mixed with ½ teaspoon of honey and 1 teaspoon of aloe vera juice, taken twice a day, can bring relief.
3. For cough and breathlessness, a pinch of cardamom, a pinch of rock salt, 1 teaspoon of ghee and ½ teaspoon of honey mixed together and licked from a spoon can be helpful.
4. For burning urination, take 1 pinch of cardamom and ½ cup of cucumber juice 2 times a day for relief.
5. Nausea can be helped with 2 pinches of cardamom and ½ teaspoon of honey, mixed with ½ cup of yogurt.
6. Eating 2 pinches of cardamom with oatmeal or cornmeal porridge will help prevent cavities in the teeth.
7. Drinking coffee is very stressful to the adrenal glands, so if you do drink coffee, a pinch of ginger and cardamom can help to neutralize this effect.

Cinnamon is sweet, pungent, bitter and heating with a pungent vipaka. It pacifies vata and kapha, but may stimulate pitta in excess. It is effective in

digestion, toxic (ama) conditions and improves circulation. It helps to prevent heart attacks owing to its blood thinning properties.

1. For common cold, cough or congestion, mix ½ teaspoon cinnamon and 1 teaspoon honey. Eat this 2 or 3 times a day.
2. For sinus headache, try ½ teaspoon cinnamon with sufficient water to make a paste and apply it locally.
3. For diarrhea, ½ cup yogurt, ½ teaspoon cinnamon and a pinch of nutmeg taken 2 or 3 times a day may help.
4. To aid poor circulation, lower high cholesterol and relieve asthma, drink a tea of 1 teaspoon cinnamon, ¼ teaspoon trikatu, 1 teaspoon honey and 1 cup hot water. Steep for 10 minutes. Take twice a day.

Clove is pungent and heating, and its vipaka is sweet. Its pungency increases pitta, but decreases vata and kapha. It is a good digestive stimulant and acts on sinus and bronchial congestion.

1. For cold or cough, try 1 teaspoon of honey mixed with a pinch of clove, 2 or 3 times a day.
2. For indigestion and low appetite, try 1 pinch of clove powder, ¼ teaspoon trikatu and 1 teaspoon of honey 5 minutes before food.
3. Hoarseness of voice can be helped by a pinch each of clove and cardamom powder, ½ teaspoon ground licorice root and 1 teaspoon of honey mixed well together and eaten slowly.
4. For diarrhea, a pinch each of clove, saffron and nutmeg powders mixed into ½ cup of yogurt and taken twice a day, will help.
5. When you have a bad toothache, try a drop of clove oil on the tooth.

Coriander is sweet, astringent and cooling with a sweet vipaka. It is tridoshic. It has good digestive properties, can reduce fever and is diuretic.
Note: The suggestions that follow are for the seed, but the coriander plant (cilantro) has similar and less strong effects.

1. For burning sensation in the urethra or for excessive thirst, take 1 teaspoon of coriander seeds and ½ teaspoon each of amalaki and natural sugar in 1 cup boiling water. Steep overnight and drink it first thing the next morning.
2. For fever, try ½ teaspoon each of coriander and cinnamon and ¼ teaspoon ginger. Steep this in 1 cup of hot water for 10 minutes before drinking.
3. For kidney stones and scanty, burning urination, steep 1 teaspoon of coriander and ½ teaspoon gokshura in 1 cup of heated rice wash

water—that is, the water from washing raw rice. Drink this 2 times a day.

4. High pitta conditions like rash, hives and nausea can be relieved by steeping 1 teaspoon of coriander, ½ teaspoon of cumin and 1 teaspoon of natural sugar in 1 cup of hot milk. Drink this once or twice a day.

5. For conjunctivitis, try the following eye wash. Steep 1 teaspoon of coriander seeds in 1 cup of boiling water for at least 15 minutes. Strain well and cool. Wash the eye with this tea. This will keep in the refrigerator for 2 or 3 days.

6. For coughing, 1 teaspoon each of coriander seed powder and natural sugar mixed in 1 cup of rice wash water—that is, the water from washing raw rice—can help.

7. A tea made from equal portions of cumin seeds, coriander seeds and fennel seeds is an excellent digestant. Use about 1 teaspoon of this mixture per cup and steep for 10 minutes.

Cumin is an aromatic seed that can be used by all doshas. Cumin is a vital part of Ayurvedic cooking, because of its distinctive taste and wonderful medicinal qualities. For any digestive complaints, one might almost say, "Just close your eyes and use cumin!" Cumin kindles the gastric fire and improves the absorption of minerals in the intestines. It helps relieve problems of gas and can also act as a mild pain reliever. Stomach pain, nausea and diarrhea can be relieved by cumin. Cumin is also very restorative to the tissues. It is pungent, bitter, and cooling with a pungent vipaka. The less common black variety is heating.

1. To bring down fever, mix equal quantities of cumin seeds, coriander seeds and fennel seeds. Add 1 teaspoon of this mixture to 1 cup boiling water. Steep for 10 minutes and drink.

2. For stomach pain, make a mixture of ⅓ teaspoon cumin powder, a pinch of hing and a pinch of rock salt. Mix and chew very well. Follow with warm water.

3. For nausea or upset stomach, a tea made from 1 teaspoon cumin seeds and a pinch of ground nutmeg in 1 cup boiling water and steeped for 10 minutes can bring some relief.

4. For vaginal infections, such as leukorrhea (white discharge), try the following: 1 teaspoon cumin seeds, 1 teaspoon *ghee*, 1 teaspoon chopped licorice root and 1 pint boiling water. Let this steep at least 10

minutes. Cool to body temperature, strain and use as a douche.
5. For some relief from menstrual pain, roast cumin seeds in an ungreased iron pan until they smell pungent. Chew a spoonful slowly, followed by 1 tablespoon aloe vera juice.

Fennel is sweet, astringent and cooling with a sweet vipaka. It is unctuous and calms all three doshas. It acts as a digestive aid and as a diuretic. It helps to get rid of intestinal worms and can relieve hemorrhoids.
1. For indigestion, chew ½ teaspoon roasted fennel and cumin seeds after each meal.
2. For acute diarrhea, mix ½ teaspoon each of fennel powder and ginger powder, and chew this 2 or 3 times a day.
3. For acute cold, cough and upper respiratory congestion, try chewing ½ teaspoon fennel seed powder mixed with 1 teaspoon of natural sugar, 2 or 3 times a day.
4. For edema, try fennel tea made from 1 teaspoon fennel seeds steeped in 1 cup boiling water, 2 times a day.
5. In cases of burning urination, drink fennel tea with 1 teaspoon natural sugar.

Ginger Fresh ginger root is pungent and heating and has a sweet vipaka. Although it is tridosha balancing, pitta individuals should use it in moderation. Dry ginger, on the other hand, is pungent and heating with a pungent vipaka. It calms vata and kapha but may stimulate pitta more than fresh ginger. This change in the action of ginger is due to the different post-digestive effects of the two types of ginger.
Both types of ginger kindle digestive fire and improve digestion, absorption and assimilation of foodstuff. Ginger can improve circulation, relieve congestion, help break down blood clots and may aid in preventing heart attacks. It is a good domestic remedy for the common cold, cough and breathlessness.
1. If one chews a thin slice of fresh ginger with a pinch of salt, 10 minutes before the meal, it acts as an appetizer and stimulates *agni*.
2. Taking a mixture of 1 teaspoon each of fresh ginger juice and lime juice, after food, aids digestion. This recipe also helps to relieve excess gas, constipation and lower abdominal pain.
3. A mixture of 1 teaspoon each of ginger juice and fresh onion juice is

good to settle down nausea and vomiting.

4. Rubbing a little fresh ginger juice around the belly button, will help stop diarrhea and abdominal pain.

5. A mixture of 1 teaspoon each of fresh ginger juice and honey, taken 2 or 3 times a day, is quite useful for sinus congestion.

6. For cold, cough, congestion and flu symptoms, 1 cup of tea made with 1 teaspoon each of dry ginger, cinnamon and fennel is beneficial.

7. A mixture of 1 teaspoon each of ginger juice and lime juice, and 2 pinches of rock salt helps relieve hoarseness of the voice, chest pain, wheezing and coughing.

8. An application of ½ teaspoon dry ginger powder paste on the forehead helps a sinus headache. Pitta individuals should be careful with this, as it may cause a slight burning of the skin. Always wash the area after treatment.

9. For jet lag, swallow 1 "00" size capsule of dry ginger powder an hour before flight.

10. Half a teaspoon of trikatu (the mixture of equal parts dry ginger, black pepper and pippali) with 1 teaspoon of honey is very good for burning ama (toxins) and excess kapha in the lungs and for regulating cholesterol and obesity. Take 2 or 3 times a day before meals.

11. To help with rheumatoid arthritis, add ½ ounce of castor oil to 1 cup of ginger tea and take before bedtime.

12. Cook 1 tablespoon of ginger powder with 2 tablespoons of ghee in an iron pot to make it into a paste. Eat ½ teaspoon at a time, 3 times a day, to help relieve diarrhea, splenic pain and osteoarthritis.

Mustard Seed Brown or black mustard seeds are pungent and heating, with a pungent vipaka. They calm vata and kapha, but provoke pitta in excess. The most powerful action of mustard seeds is to assist in healing the bronchial system. Mustard seeds are very helpful with sprains and pains or to help get rid of intestinal worms. Mustard is also a digestive.

Mustard oil is strongly aromatic and heating, so it is best to use it in cold climates. It will cover up all other tastes when you cook with it. Yellow mustard seeds have similar properties but are milder.

1. For bronchial asthma, try taking 1 teaspoon of brown mustard oil mixed with 1 teaspoon of natural sugar, 2 or 3 times a day on an empty stomach. Or try a tea made from ¼ teaspoon each of ground mustard seeds and pippali or black pepper with 1 to 2 teaspoons of honey, 2 or 3

times a day. Rubbing mustard oil on the chest also can give some relief.

2. For persistent cough, mix ½ teaspoon each of ground mustard seeds and ginger powder with 1 teaspoon of honey and eat it slowly, 2 to 3 times a day.

3. For itching of the skin, apply mustard oil to the area an hour before bathing. Do not use on very sensitive tissue such as genitals or nipples.

4. For ankle sprain, muscular or arthritic pain, or edema in the legs, soak the feet or hands in a large pot of hot water with a mustard seed tea bag—2 teaspoons of seeds tied up in some cotton or cheesecloth— immersed in it. Rubbing mustard oil on sore arthritic joints will help dissolve the crystals that cause the friction.

5. A poultice made from mustard seed pulp spread on a piece of thick cotton is good to put on the site of muscle pain. Don't put the seeds next to your skin.

6. The poultice mentioned above also helps to reduce the pain and size of an enlarged spleen.

7. For intestinal worms, make a mixture of 1 teaspoon ground mustard seed, ½ teaspoon of cayenne and a very small pinch of hing. Put this into "00" size capsules and take 1 after each meal for 15 days. To calm pitta, take 1 tablespoon of aloe vera juice with each one. Take for 15 days. This formula can also be used for your pets.

Nutmeg is sweet, astringent, pungent, heating and the vipaka is pungent. It has a pleasant smell. It increases pitta and decreases vata and kapha. It improves the flavor of food. It is good for digestion, helps relieve cough, induces sleep and can reduce pain.

1. For headache, apply a paste of a pinch of nutmeg and water to the affected area.

2. For insomnia, a fine paste of nutmeg with an equal amount of ghee, applied around the eyes and forehead before bed, can help. Also drink 1 cup of hot milk and a pinch of nutmeg before bed. This may produce a little constipation, so drink a cup of triphala tea the next morning—½ teaspoon steeped in 1 cup boiling water.

3. For diarrhea, try mixing ⅓ teaspoon of nutmeg and 1 teaspoon of warm ghee, and slowly eat this from a spoon 2 to 3 times a day.

4. In cases of nausea and morning sickness during pregnancy, take a pinch each of nutmeg and cardamom in ½ cup warm milk.

5. For relief from arthritic pain, try rubbing nutmeg oil on the joint.

Saffron is sweet, astringent and heating, and has a sweet vipaka. It is tridosha balancing and is good for improving skin color and complexion. Some of its many uses are as a blood cleanser, liver detoxifier, nerve tonic, blood thinner and as a heart tonic. It is aphrodisiac and can help increase the sperm count. It can also be used for cough, cold, congestion and hemorrhoids.

1. For sexual debility, drink 1 cup hot milk with a pinch of saffron.
2. For hemorrhoids, take internally a pinch of saffron, ¼ teaspoon of triphala and 1 tablespoon aloe vera gel 2 times a day.
3. For relief from some of the symptoms of asthma and cough, mix a pinch of saffron, ½ teaspoon of trikatu and 1 teaspoon of honey. Take this 2 or 3 times a day.
4. For heart palpitation and chest pain, boil ½ cup each of milk and water, 2 pinches of saffron and ½ teaspoon of arjuna. Drink this 2 or 3 times a day.
5. As a brain tonic, try drinking a pinch of saffron and ½ teaspoon of brahmi (gotu kola), boiled in 1 cup of milk.
6. Rosewater and saffron water—soak a pinch of saffron in ¼ cup of water for at least 15 minutes—diluted in distilled water to a 1 percent solution can help conjunctivitis and burning eyes. Put 2 drops in each eye.

Salt is heating, it increases pitta and kapha, and decreases vata. Sea salt has a pungent vipaka. Salt is a digestant and improves the flavor of food. It is laxative and antiseptic and can be used to induce vomiting. Rock salt is a mineral salt that is very digestive. It has a special flavor, a sweet vipaka and is not quite so aggravating to pitta and kapha. It does not retain water in the body.

1. For sinus headache and congestion, mix ½ teaspoon of salt in ½ cup of warm water. Put 5 drops in each nostril. This will help drain the sinuses.
2. For feelings of nausea or for headache and cold, drink a pint of salt water—2 teaspoons in 1 pint of water—in the early morning, then rub the tongue to induce vomiting.
3. Drinking 1 cup of water with 1 teaspoon of salt may induce loose bowel movements and relieve constipation.
4. For dizziness due to over-sweating, drink a glass of water with a small pinch of salt and ½ teaspoon of lime juice.
5. Salt can relieve edema and swelling resulting from a sprained ankle.

Soak the foot for 15 minutes in hot water with 2 tablespoons of salt per gallon of water.

6. One part salt and 2 parts turmeric with sufficient water to make a paste applied to the site of an injury will help reduce swelling.

7. For a sore throat and laryngitis, gargle at night with 1 cup of hot water, ½ teaspoon salt and 1 teaspoon of turmeric.

Tulsi *(Indian basil or holy basil)* is sweet, pungent, astringent and heating with a pungent vipaka. It increases pitta, and decreases vata and kapha. It has a refreshing, pleasant smell, so keeping a plant in your house can purify the air. It is good for fever, cough and breathlessness.

Note: The basil we are familiar with in North America has somewhat similar properties but is less potent.

1. For flu, make a tea from 1 teaspoon of basil in 1 cup of water. Boil it for just a minute and drink.

2. For chronic fever, make basil tea with a pinch of black pepper. Drink 2 to 3 times a day.

3. For common cold, cough and sinus congestion, steep ¼ teaspoon each of basil and dry ginger and ½ teaspoon of cinnamon in 1 cup of hot water. Take 2 or 3 times a day.

4. For ulcerative colitis, take 1 teaspoon of basil seeds and soak them overnight in a cup of water. Drain and mix the seeds with ½ cup yogurt. Take this in the morning.

5. For nausea and vomiting, mix 1 teaspoon fresh basil juice with 1 teaspoon of honey and eat twice a day.

Turmeric Fresh turmeric root looks a little like ginger, but inside it can be red or yellow. The red is called kunkum and is considered sacred. Only the yellow root is used in cooking and medicinally.

Turmeric is the best medicine in Ayurveda. It cures the whole person. Turmeric is pungent, bitter, astringent and heating and has a pungent vipaka. Turmeric can be used by all doshas. It may stimulate vata, but doesn't aggravate it (cause an imbalance). Turmeric helps digestion, maintains the flora of the intestine, reduces gas, has tonic properties and is an antibiotic. Turmeric can be used for cough, sty, diabetes, hemorrhoids, cuts, wounds, burns and skin problems. It helps reduce anxiety and stress.

Note: People with hypoglycemia can use small amounts of turmeric in cooking but should not take it in quantity.

GENTLE REMINDER: The yellow color of turmeric tends to stain your clothes and skin.

1. For bronchial cough, dry sore throat, tonsillitis and pharyngitis, drink at bedtime 1 cup of hot milk and 1 teaspoon of turmeric boiled together for 3 minutes.

2. For external hemorrhoids, apply a mixture of ½ teaspoon of turmeric and 1 teaspoon of ghee locally at bedtime.

3. For fibrocystic breast, apply a paste of ½ teaspoon turmeric powder and 1 teaspoon warm castor oil on the breast at night. (Just a reminder: it will turn the skin yellow, and the clothes too.)

4. To help stabilize blood sugar in diabetes, put turmeric powder in "00" size capsules. Swallow 2 capsules 3 times a day, 5 minutes before each meal.

5. For anemia, take a bowl of yogurt with up to 1 teaspoon of turmeric. Eat on an empty stomach morning and afternoon. Do not eat after sunset. If kapha is unbalanced, eat this at noon only.

6. For cuts, wound and fungal nail infections, apply a mixture of ½ teaspoon turmeric and 1 teaspoon aloe vera gel to the affected area.

7. For swelling from traumatic injury, apply a paste of turmeric and water.

8. For a sty in the eye, make a paste of equal parts of red sandalwood powder and turmeric mixed with distilled water. Place on the eyelid to drain the sty.

9. Apply turmeric directly to the affected area of the mouth in cases of swollen gums and canker sores.

10. For beautiful skin take a turmeric capsule daily. If a pregnant woman takes turmeric regularly, her child will have gorgeous skin.

11. If there is a family history of melanoma, take 1 or 2 turmeric capsules 3 times a day to help as a preventative.

12. For a sun block for moles, cover them with a mixture of 2 parts ghee and 1 part turmeric.

13. For general protection from disease, carry turmeric root in your pocket or tie it on a yellow silk thread around your neck.

Appendix

Determining Your Constitution

To determine your constitution it is best to fill out twice the chart that follows. First base your choices on what is most consistent over a long period of your life, your prakruti, then fill it out a second time responding to how you have been feeling recently in the last month or two, your vikruti. Sometimes it helps to have a friend ask you the questions and fill in the chart for you, as they may have reliable insight and impartiality to offer.

 After finishing the chart, add up the number of marks under vata, pitta and kapha to discover your own balance of doshas in your prakruti and vikruti. Most people will have one dosha predominant, a few will have two doshas approximately equal and even fewer will have all three doshas in equal proportion. For instance, if your vikruti shows more pitta than your prakruti, you will want to follow a pitta soothing diet to try and lower your pitta principle. If your prakruti and vikruti seem about the same, then you would choose the diet of your strongest dosha. If you have a kapha disorder at the moment, like sinus congestion, you may want to eat a kapha soothing diet until it disappears.

Guidelines For Determining Your Constitution

OBSERVATIONS	V	P	K	VATA	PITTA	KAPHA
Body size	☐	☐	☐	Slim	Medium	Large
Body weight	☐	☐	☐	Low	Medium	Overweight
Skin	☐	☐	☐	Thin, Dry, Cold, Rough, Dark	Smooth, Oily, Warm, Rosy	Thick, Oily, Cool, White, Pale
Hair	☐	☐	☐	Dry, Brown, Black, Knotted, Brittle, Thin	Straight, Oily, Blond, Grey, Red, Bald	Thick, Curly, Oily, Wavy, Luxuriant, All colors
Teeth	☐	☐	☐	Protruding, Big, Roomy, Thin gums	Medium, Soft, Tender gums	Healthy, White, Strong gums
Nose	☐	☐	☐	Uneven shape, Deviated septum	Long pointed, Red nose-tip	Short Rounded, Button nose
Eyes	☐	☐	☐	Small, Sunken, Dry, Active, Black, Brown, Nervous	Sharp, Bright, Grey, Green, Yellow/red, Sensitive to light	Big, beautiful, Blue, Calm, Loving
Nails	☐	☐	☐	Dry, Rough, Brittle, Break easily	Sharp, Flexible, Pink, Lustrous	Thick, Oily, Smooth, Polished
Lips	☐	☐	☐	Dry, Cracked, Black/brown tinged	Red, Inflamed, Yellowish	Smooth, Oily, Pale, Whitish
Chin	☐	☐	☐	Thin, Angular	Tapering	Rounded, Double
Cheeks	☐	☐	☐	Wrinkled, Sunken	Smooth Flat	Rounded, Plump
Neck	☐	☐	☐	Thin, Tall	Medium	Big, Folded
Chest	☐	☐	☐	Flat, Sunken	Moderate	Expanded, Round
Belly	☐	☐	☐	Thin, Flat, Sunken	Moderate	Big, Potbellied
Belly-button	☐	☐	☐	Small, Irregular, Herniated	Oval, Superficial	Big, Deep, Round, Stretched
Hips	☐	☐	☐	Slender, Thin	Moderate	Heavy, Big
Joints	☐	☐	☐	Cold, Cracking	Moderate	Large, Lubricated

Appetite	☐ Irregular, Scanty	☐ Strong, Unbearable	☐ Slow but steady
Digestion	☐ Irregular, Forms gas	☐ Quick, Causes burning	☐ Prolonged, Forms mucous
Taste, healthy preference	☐ Sweet, Sour, Salty	☐ Sweet, Bitter, Astringent	☐ Bitter, Pungent, Astringent
Thirst	☐ Changeable	☐ Surplus	☐ Sparse
Elimination	☐ Constipation	☐ Loose	☐ Thick, Oily, Sluggish
Physical Activity	☐ Hyperactive	☐ Moderate	☐ Sedentary
Mental Activity	☐ Always Active	☐ Moderate	☐ Dull, Slow
Emotions	☐ Anxiety, Fear, Uncertainty, Flexible	☐ Anger, Hate, Jealousy, Determined	☐ Calm, Greedy, Attachment
Faith	☐ Variable, Changeable	☐ Intense, Extremist	☐ Consistent, Deep, Mellow
Intellect	☐ Quick but faulty response	☐ Accurate response	☐ Slow, Exact
Recollection	☐ Recent good, remote poor	☐ Distinct	☐ Slow and sustained
Dreams	☐ Quick, Active, Many, Fearful,	☐ Fiery, War, Violence	☐ Lakes, Snow, Romantic
Sleep	☐ Scanty, Broken up, Sleeplessness	☐ Little but sound	☐ Deep, Prolonged
Speech	☐ Rapid, Unclear	☐ Sharp, Penetrating	☐ Slow, monotonous
Financial	☐ Poor, spends on trifles	☐ Spends money on luxuries	☐ Rich, Good money preserver
TOTAL			

Food Guidelines for Basic Constitutional Types

NOTE: *Guidelines provided in this table are general. Specific adjustments for individual requirements may need to be made, e.g., food allergies, strength of agni, season of the year and degree of dosha predominance or aggravation.* * okay in moderation ** okay rarely

	VATA AVOID	VATA FAVOR	PITTA AVOID	PITTA FAVOR	KAPHA AVOID	KAPHA FAVOR
FRUITS	Generally most dried fruit	Generally most sweet fruit	Generally most sour fruit	Generally most sweet fruit	Generally most sweet & sour fruit	Generally most astringent fruit
	Apples (raw)	Apples (cooked)	Apples (sour)	Apples (sweet)	Avocado	Apples
	Cranberries	Applesauce	Apricots (sour)	Applesauce	Bananas	Applesauce
	Dates (dry)	Apricots	Bananas	Apricots (sweet)	Coconut	Apricots
	Figs (dry)	Avocado	Berries (sour)	Avocado	Dates	Berries
	Pears	Bananas	Cherries (sour)	Berries (sweet)	Figs (fresh)	Cherries
	Persimmons	Berries	Cranberries	Cherries (sweet)	Grapefruit	Cranberries
	Pomegranates	Cherries	Grapefruit	Coconut	Kiwi	Figs (dry)*
	Raisins (dry)	Coconut	Grapes (green)	Dates	Mangos**	Grapes*
	Prunes (dry)	Dates (fresh)	Kiwi**	Figs	Melons	Lemons*
	Watermelon	Figs (fresh)	Lemons	Grapes (red & purple)	Oranges	Limes*
		Grapefruit	Mangoes (green)	Limes*	Papaya	Peaches*
		Grapes	Oranges (sour)	Mangoes (ripe)	Pineapple	Pears
		Kiwi	Peaches	Melons	Plums	Persimmons
		Lemons	Persimmons	Oranges (sweet)*	Rhubarb	Pomegranates
		Limes	Pineapple (sour)	Papaya*	Tamarind	Prunes
		Mangoes	Plums (sour)	Pears	Watermelon	Raisins
		Melons	Rhubarb	Pineapple (sweet)*		Strawberries*
		Oranges	Tamarind	Plums (sweet)		
		Papaya		Pomegranates		
		Peaches		Prunes		
		Pineapple		Raisins		
		Plums		Strawberries*		
		Prunes (soaked)		Watermelon		
		Raisins (soaked)				
		Rhubarb				
		Strawberries				
		Tamarind				

VEGETABLES

Generally frozen, raw or dried vegetables	In general, vegetables should be cooked	In general, pungent vegetables	In general, sweet & bitter vegetables	In general, sweet & juicy vegetables	In general, most pungent & bitter vegetables
Artichoke	Asparagus	Beet greens	Artichoke	Cucumber	Artichoke
Beet greens**	Beets	Beets (raw)	Asparagus	Olives, black or green	Asparagus
Bitter melon	Cabbage*	Burdock root	Beets (cooked)	Parsnips**	Beet greens
Broccoli	Carrots	Corn (fresh)**	Bitter melon	Potatoes, sweet	Beets
Brussels sprouts	Cauliflower*	Daikon radish	Broccoli	Pumpkin	Bitter melon
Burdock root	Cilantro	Eggplant**	Brussels sprouts	Squash, summer	Broccoli
Cabbage (raw)	Cucumber	Garlic	Cabbage	Taro root	Brussels sprouts
Cauliflower (raw)	Daikon radish*	Green chilies	Carrots (cooked)	Tomatoes (raw)	Burdock root
Celery	Fennel	Horseradish	Carrots (raw)*	Zucchini	Cabbage
Corn (fresh)**	Garlic	Kohlrabi **	Cauliflower		Carrots
Dandelion greens	Green beans	Leeks (raw)	Celery		Cauliflower
Eggplant	Green chilies	Mustard greens	Cilantro		Celery
Horseradish**	Jerusalem artichoke*	Olives, green	Cucumber		Cilantro
Kale	Leafy greens*	Onions (raw)	Dandelion greens		Corn
Kohlrabi	Leeks	Peppers (hot)	Fennel		Daikon radish
Mushrooms	Lettuce*	Prickly pear (fruit)	Green beans		Dandelion greens
Olives, green	Mustard greens*	Radishes (raw)	Jerusalem artichoke		Eggplant
Onions (raw)	Okra	Spinach (cooked)**	Kale		Fennel
Peas (raw)	Olives, black	Spinach (raw)	Leafy greens		Garlic
Peppers, sweet & hot	Onions (cooked)*	Tomatoes	Leeks (cooked)		Green beans
Potatoes, white	Parsley*	Turnip greens	Lettuce		Green chilies
Prickly pear (fruit & leaves)	Parsnip	Turnips	Mushrooms		Horseradish
Radish (raw)	Peas (cooked)		Okra		Jerusalem artichoke
Squash, winter	Potatoes, sweet		Olives, black		Kale
Tomatoes (cooked)**	Pumpkin		Onions (cooked)		Kohlrabi
Tomatoes (raw)**	Radishes (cooked)*		Parsley		Leafy greens
Turnips	Rutabaga		Parsnips		Leeks
Wheat grass sprouts	Spaghetti squash*		Peas		Lettuce
	Spinach (cooked)*		Peppers, sweet		Mushrooms
	Spinach (raw)*		Potatoes, sweet & white		Mustard greens
					Okra
					Onions

221

	VATA		PITTA		KAPHA	
	AVOID	FAVOR	AVOID	FAVOR	AVOID	FAVOR
VEGETABLES		Sprouts* Squash, summer Taro root Turnip greens* Watercress Zucchini		Prickly pear (leaves) Pumpkin Radishes (cooked) Rutabaga Spaghetti squash Sprouts (not spicy) Squash, winter & summer Taro root Watercress* Wheat grass sprouts Zucchini		Parsley Peas Peppers, sweet & hot Potatoes, white Prickly pear (fruit & leaves) Radishes Rutabaga Spaghetti squash* Spinach Sprouts Squash, winter Tomatoes (cooked) Turnip greens Turnips Watercress Wheat grass
GRAINS	Barley Bread (with yeast) Buckwheat Cereals (cold, dry or puffed) Corn Couscous Crackers Granola Millet Muesli Oat bran Oats (dry)	Amaranth* Durham flour Oats (cooked) Pancakes Quinoa Rice (all kinds) Seitan (wheat meat) Sprouted wheat bread (Essene) Wheat	Bread (with yeast) Buckwheat Corn Millet** Muesli** Oats (dry) Polenta** Rice (brown)** Rye	Amaranth Barley Cereal, dry Couscous Crackers Durham flour Granola Oat bran Oats (cooked) Pancakes Pasta Quinoa	Bread (with yeast) Oats (cooked) Pancakes Pasta** Rice (brown, white) Rice cakes** Wheat	Amaranth* Barley Buckwheat Cereal (cold, dry or puffed) Corn Couscous Crackers Durham flour* Granola Millet Muesli Oat bran

Pasta**		Rice (basmati, white, wild)		Oats (dry)	
Polenta**		Rice cakes		Polenta	
Rice cakes**		Seitan (wheat meat)		Quinoa*	
Rye		Spelt		Rice (basmati, wild)*	
Sago		Sprouted wheat bread (Essene)		Rye	
Spelt		Tapioca		Seitan (wheat meat)	
Tapioca		Wheat		Spelt*	
Wheat bran		Wheat bran		Sprouted wheat bread (Essene)	
				Tapioca	
				Wheat bran	

LEGUMES	Aduki beans	Lentils (red)*	Aduki beans	Miso	Aduki beans	Kidney beans
	Black beans	Mung beans	Black beans	Soy sauce	Black beans	Soy beans
	Black-eyed peas	Mung dal	Black-eyed peas	Soy sausages	Black-eyed peas	Soy cheese
	Chick peas (garbanzo beans)	Soy cheese*	Chick peas (garbanzo beans)	Tur dal	Chick peas (garbanzo beans)	Soy flour
	Kidney beans	Soy milk*	Kidney beans	Urad dal	Lentils red & brown	Soy powder
	Lentils (brown)	Soy sauce*	Lentils, brown & red		Lima beans	Soy sauce
	Lima beans	Soy sausages*	Lima beans		Mung beans*	Tofu (cold)
	Miso**	Tofu*	Mung beans		Mung dal*	Urad dal
	Navy beans	Tur dal	Mung dal		Navy beans	Miso
	Peas (dried)	Urad dal	Navy beans		Peas (dried)	
	Pinto beans		Peas (dried)		Pinto beans	
	Soy beans		Pinto beans		Soy milk	
	Soy flour		Soy beans		Soy sausages	
	Soy powder		Soy cheese		Split peas	
	Split peas		Soy flour*		Tempeh	
	Tempeh		Soy milk		Tofu (hot)*	
	White beans		Soy powder*		Tur dal	
			Split peas		White beans	

223

	VATA		PITTA		KAPHA	
	AVOID	FAVOR	AVOID	FAVOR	AVOID	FAVOR
LEGUMES				Tempeh Tofu White beans		
DAIRY	Cow's milk (powdered) Goat's milk (powdered) Yogurt (plain, frozen or w/ fruit)	Most dairy is good! Butter (unsalted) Buttermilk Butter (salted) Cheese (hard)* Cheese (soft) Cottage cheese Cow's milk Ghee Goat's cheese Goat's milk Ice cream* Sour cream* Yogurt (diluted & spiced)*	Butter (salted) Buttermilk Cheese (hard) Sour cream Yogurt (plain, frozen or w/fruit)	Butter (unsalted) Cheese (soft, not aged, unsalted) Cottage cheese Cow's milk Ghee Goat's milk Goat's cheese (soft, unsalted) Ice cream Yogurt (freshly made & diluted)*	Butter (salted) Butter (unsalted)** Cheese (soft & hard) Cow's milk Ice cream Sour cream Yogurt (plain, frozen or w/fruit)	Buttermilk* Cottage cheese (from skimmed goat's milk) Ghee* Goat's cheese (unsalted & not aged)* Goat's milk, skim Yogurt (diluted)
ANIMAL FOODS	Lamb Pork Rabbit Venison Turkey (white)	Beef Buffalo Chicken (dark) Chicken (white)* Duck Eggs Fish (freshwater or sea) Salmon Sardines Seafood Shrimp	Beef Chicken (dark) Duck Eggs (yolk) Fish (sea) Lamb Pork Salmon Sardines Seafood Tuna fish Turkey (dark)	Buffalo Chicken (white) Eggs (albumen or white only) Fish (freshwater) Rabbit Shrimp* Turkey (white) Venison	Beef Buffalo Chicken (dark) Duck Fish (sea) Lamb Pork Salmon Sardines Seafood Tuna fish Turkey (dark)	Chicken (white) Eggs Fish (freshwater) Rabbit Shrimp Turkey (white) Venison

	Tuna fish / Turkey (dark)					
CONDIMENTS	Chocolate Horseradish	Black pepper* Chutney, mango (sweet or spicy) Chili peppers* Coriander leaves* Dulse Gomasio Hijiki Kelp Ketchup Kombu Lemon Lime Lime pickle Mango pickle Mayonnaise Mustard Pickles Salt Scallions Seaweed Soy sauce Sprouts* Tamari Vinegar	Chili pepper Chocolate Chutney, mango (spicy) Gomasio Horseradish Kelp Ketchup Mustard Lemon Lime pickle Mango pickle Mayonnaise Pickles Salt (in excess) Scallions Soy sauce Vinegar	Black pepper* Chutney, mango (sweet) Coriander leaves Dulse* Hijiki* Kombu* Lime* Sprouts Salt* Seaweed* Tamari*	Chocolate Chutney, mango (sweet) Gomasio Kelp Ketchup** Lime Lime pickle Mango pickle Mayonnaise Pickles Salt Soy sauce Tamari Vinegar	Black pepper Chili Peppers Chutney, mango (spicy) Coriander leaves Dulse* Hijiki* Horseradish Lemon* Mustard (without vinegar) Scallions Seaweed* Sprouts
NUTS	None	In moderation: Almonds Black walnuts Brazil nuts Cashews Charole Coconut	Almonds (with skin) Black walnuts Brazil nuts Cashews Filberts Hazelnuts	Almonds (soaked and peeled) Charole Coconut	Almonds (soaked and peeled)** Black walnuts Brazil nuts Cashews Coconut Filberts	Charole

225

	VATA		PITTA		KAPHA	
	AVOID	FAVOR	AVOID	FAVOR	AVOID	FAVOR
NUTS		Filberts Hazelnuts Macadamia nuts Peanuts Pecans Pine nuts Pistachios Walnuts	Macadamia nuts Peanuts Pecans Pine nuts Pistachios Walnuts		Hazelnuts Macadamia nuts Peanuts Pecans Pine nuts Pistachios Walnuts	
SEEDS	Popcorn Psyllium**	Chia Flax Halva Pumpkin Sesame Sunflower Tahini	Chia Sesame Tahini	Flax Halva Popcorn (no salt, buttered) Psyllium Pumpkin* Sunflower	Halva Psyllium** Sesame Tahini	Chia Flax* Popcorn (no salt, no butter) Pumpkin* Sunflower*
OILS	Flax seed	*For internal & external use:* *(most suitable at top of list)* Sesame Ghee Olive Most other oils *External use only:* Coconut Avocado	Almond Apricot Corn Safflower Sesame	*For internal & external use:* *(most suitable at top of list)* Sunflower Ghee Canola Olive Soy Flax seed Primrose Walnut *External use only:* Avocado Coconut	Avocado Apricot Coconut Flax seed** Olive Primrose Safflower Sesame (internal) Soy Walnut	*For internal & external use in small amounts:* *(Most suitable at top of list)* Corn Canola Sesame (external) Sunflower Ghee Almond

BEVERAGES

Alcohol (hard; red wine)	Alcohol (beer; white wine)*	Alcohol (hard; red & sweet wine)	Alcohol (beer; dry white wine)*	Alcohol (hard; beer; sweet wine)	Alcohol (dry wine, red or white)*
Apple juice	Almond milk	Apple cider	Almond milk	Almond milk	Aloe vera juice
Black tea	Aloe vera juice	Berry juice (sour)	Aloe vera juice	Caffeinated beverages**	Apple cider
Caffeinated beverages	Apple cider	Caffeinated beverages	Apple juice	Carbonated drinks	Apple juice*
Carbonated drinks	Apricot juice	Carbonated drinks	Apricot juice	Cherry juice (sour)	Apricot juice
Chocolate milk	Berry juice (except for cranberry)	Carrot juice	Berry juice (sweet)	Chocolate milk	Berry juice
Coffee	Carob*	Cherry juice (sour)	Black tea*	Coffee	Black tea (spiced)
Cold dairy drinks	Carrot juice	Chocolate milk	Carob	Cold dairy drinks	Carob
Cranberry juice	Chai (hot spiced milk)	Coffee	Chai (hot, spiced milk)*	Grapefruit juice	Carrot juice
Iced tea	Cherry juice	Cranberry juice	Cherry juice (sweet)	Iced tea	Chai (hot, spiced milk)*
Icy cold drinks	Grain "coffee"	Grapefruit juice	Cool dairy drinks	Icy cold drinks	Cherry juice (sweet)
Pear juice	Grape juice	Iced tea	Grain "coffee"	Lemonade	Cranberry juice
Pomegranate juice	Grapefruit juice	Icy cold drinks	Grape juice	Miso broth	Grain "coffee"
Prune juice**	Lemonade	Lemonade	Mango juice	Orange juice	Grape juice
Soy milk (cold)	Mango juice	Papaya juice	Miso broth*	Papaya juice	Mango juice
Tomato juice**	Miso broth	Pineapple juice	Mixed veg. juice	Rice milk	Peach nectar
V-8 Juice	Orange juice	Tomato juice	Orange juice*	Sour juices	Pear juice
	Papaya juice	V-8 juice	Peach nectar	Soy milk (cold)	Pineapple juice*
	Peach nectar	Sour juices	Pear juice	Tomato juice	Pomegranate juice
	Pineapple juice		Pomegranate juice	V-8 Juice	Prune juice
	Rice milk		Prune juice		Soy milk (hot & well-spiced)
	Sour juices		Rice milk		
	Soy milk (hot & well-spiced)*		Soy milk		
	Vegetable bouillon		Vegetable bouillon		

HERBAL TEAS

Alfalfa**	Ajwan	Ajwan	Alfalfa	Licorice**	Alfalfa
Barley**	Bancha	Basil**	Bancha	Marshmallow	Bancha
Basil**	Catnip*	Clove	Barley	Red Zinger	Barley
Blackberry	Chamomile	Eucalyptus	Blackberry	Rosehip**	Blackberry
Borage**	Chicory*	Fenugreek	Borage		Burdock
Burdock	Chrysanthemum*	Ginger (dry)	Burdock		Chamomile
Cinnamon**	Clove	Ginseng	Catnip		Chicory

	VATA		PITTA		KAPHA	
	AVOID	FAVOR	AVOID	FAVOR	AVOID	FAVOR
HERBAL TEAS	Cornsilk	Comfrey	Hawthorne	Chamomile		Cinnamon
	Dandelion	Elder Flower	Juniper berry	Chicory		Clove
	Ginseng	Eucalyptus	Mormon tea	Comfrey		Comfrey*
	Hibiscus	Fennel	Pennyroyal	Dandelion		Dandelion
	Hops**	Fenugreek	Red Zinger	Fennel		Fennel*
	Jasmine**	Ginger (fresh)	Rosehip**	Ginger (fresh)		Fenugreek
	Lemon balm**	Hawthorne	Sage	Hibiscus		Ginger
	Mormon tea	Juniper berry	Sassafras	Hops		Ginseng*
	Nettle**	Kukicha*	Yerba Mate	Jasmine		Hibiscus
	Passion flower**	Lavender		Kukicha		Jasmine
	Red clover**	Lemon grass		Lavender		Juniper berry
	Red Zinger**	Licorice		Lemon balm		Kukicha
	Violet**	Marshmallow		Lemon grass		Lavender
	Yarrow	Oat straw		Licorice		Lemon balm
	Yerba Mate**	Orange peel		Marshmallow		Lemon grass
		Pennyroyal		Nettle		Mormon tea
		Peppermint		Oat Straw		Nettle
		Raspberry*		Passion flower		Passion flower
		Rosehips		Peppermint		Peppermint
		Saffron		Raspberry		Raspberry
		Sage		Red clover		Red clover
		Sarsaparilla		Sarsaparilla		Sarsaparilla*
		Sassafras		Spearmint		Sassafras
		Spearmint		Strawberry		Spearmint
		Strawberry*		Violet		Strawberry
		Wintergreen*		Wintergreen		Wintergreen
				Yarrow		Yarrow
						Yerba Mate
SPICES		All spices are good	Ajwan	Basil (fresh)	Salt	All spices are good
		Ajwan	Allspice	Black pepper*		Ajwan
		Allspice	Almond extract	Caraway*		Allspice
			Anise	Cardamom*		

Almond extract	Asafoetida (hing)	Cinnamon	Almond extract
Anise	Basil (dry)	Coriander	Anise
Asafoetida (hing)	Bay leaf	Cumin	Asafoetida (hing)
Anise	Cayenne	Dill	Basil
Asafoetida (hing)	Cloves	Fennel	Bay leaf
Basil	Fenugreek	Ginger (fresh)	Black pepper
Bay leaf	Garlic	Mint	Caraway
Black pepper	Ginger (dry)	Neem leaves*	Cardamom
Caraway	Mace	Orange peel*	Cayenne
Cardamom	Marjoram	Parsley*	Cinnamon
Cayenne*	Mustard seeds	Peppermint	Cloves
Cinnamon	Nutmeg	Saffron	Coriander
Cloves	Oregano	Spearmint	Cumin
Coriander	Paprika	Tarragon*	Dill
Cumin	Pippali	Turmeric	Fennel*
Dill	Poppy seeds	Vanilla*	Fenugreek
Fennel	Rosemary	Wintergreen	Garlic
Fenugreek*	Sage		Ginger
Garlic	Salt		Marjoram
Ginger	Savory		Mint
Marjoram	Star anise		Mustard seeds
Mint	Thyme		Neem leaves
Mustard seeds			Nutmeg
Nutmeg			Orange peel
Orange peel			Oregano
Oregano			Paprika
Paprika			Parsley
Parsley			Peppermint
Peppermint			Pippali
Pippali			Poppy seeds
Poppy seeds			Rosemary
Rosemary			Saffron
Saffron			Savory
Salt			Spearmint
Savory			Star Anise
Spearmint			Tarragon
Star anise			
Tarragon			

	VATA AVOID	VATA FAVOR	PITTA AVOID	PITTA FAVOR	KAPHA AVOID	KAPHA FAVOR
SPICES		Thyme Turmeric Vanilla Wintergreen				Thyme Turmeric Vanilla* Wintergreen
SWEETENERS	Maple syrup** White sugar	Barley malt Fructose Fruit juice concentrates Honey Jaggary Molasses Rice syrup Sucanat Turbinado	White sugar** Honey** Jaggary Molasses	Barley malt Fructose Fruit juice concentrates Maple syrup Rice syrup Sucanat Turbinado	Barley Malt Fructose Jaggary Maple syrup Molasses Rice syrup Sucanat Turbinado White sugar	Fruit juice concentrates Honey (raw & not processed)
FOOD SUPPLEMENTS	Barley green Brewer's yeast *Vitamin:* K	Aloe vera juice* Bee pollen Amino acids *Minerals:* calcium, copper, iron, magnesium, zinc Royal jelly Spirolina Blue-green algae *Vitamins:* A, B_1, B_2, B_6, B_{12}, C, D, E, P and Folic Acid	Amino acids Bee pollen** Royal jelly** *Minerals:* copper, iron *Vitamins:* B_2, B_6C, E, P and Folic Acid	Aloe vera juice Barley green Brewer's yeast *Minerals:* calcium, magnesium, zinc Spirolina Blue-green algae *Vitamins:* A, B_1, B_{12}, D and K	*Minerals:* potassium *Vitamins:* A, B_1, B_2, B_{12}, C, D and E	Aloe vera juice Amino acids Barley green Bee pollen Brewer's yeast *Minerals:* copper, calcium, iron, magnesium, zinc Royal jelly Spirolina Blue-green algae *Vitamins:* B_6, C. P and Folic Acid

How to Use the Food Guidelines

As with most things in Ayurveda, following the food guidelines is best done in moderation. Basically, these categories use the properties and qualities of each food to balance the qualities of the respective *dosha*. One can simply eat the foods in the "Favor" column and avoid the foods in the "Avoid" column to pacify the *dosha* that is aggravated. There may be times when one needs to pacify one *dosha* while trying not to aggravate one of the others. In this more difficult situation, each food choice should be in the "Favor" columns of both *doshas*. These guidelines can also be used for food choices as the seasons change.

Qualities of Food Substances

FOOD	RASA	VIRYA	VIPAKA	ACTION ON DOSHA	
FRUITS					
Apple, ripe	Astringent, Sweet, Sour	Cooling	Sweet	Rough, Light	V↑ P↓ K↓
Apple, unripe	Astringent, Sour	Cooling	Pungent	Rough, Light	V↑ P↑ K↓
Avocado	Astringent	Cooling	Sweet	Oily, Heavy, Soft	V↓ P↓ K↑
Apricots	Sweet	Heating	Sweet	Liquid, Heavy, Sour	V↓ P↑ K↓
Berries, most sour	Sour	Heating	Pungent	Sharp, Light	V↓ P↑ K↓
Berries, most sweet	Sweet	Cooling	Sweet	Unctuous, Liquid	V↓ P↓ K↓
Banana, green	Astringent	Cooling	Pungent	Soft, Light	V↑ P↓ K↓
Banana, ripe	Sweet	Heating	Sour	Smooth, Heavy	V↓ P↑ K↑
Cantaloupe	Sweet	Heating	Sweet	Heavy, Watery	V↓ P↓ K↑
Cherries	Sweet, Astringent, Sour	Heating	Pungent	Light, Liquid	V↓ P↑ K↓
Coconut	Sweet	Cooling	Sweet	Oily, Hard	V↓ P↓ K↑
Cranberries	Astringent, Sour	Heating	Pungent	Light, Dry, Sharp	V↑ P↓ K↓
Dates	Sweet	Cooling	Sweet	Heavy, Energizer	V↓ P↓ K↑
Figs	Sweet	Cooling	Sweet	Heavy, Energizer	V↓ P↓ K↑
Grapes, green	Sour, Sweet	Heating	Sweet	Liquid, Strengthening	V↓ P↑ K↑
Grapes, red/purple/black	Sweet, Sour, Astringent	Cooling	Sweet	Smooth, Energizer	V↓ P↓ K↓↑
Grapefruit	Sour	Heating	Sour	Acidic, Hydrophilic	V↓ P↑ K↑
Kiwi	Sweet, Astringent	Heating	Pungent	Heavy, Hydrophilic	V↓ P↑ K↑
Lemon	Sour	Heating	Sour	Juicy, Digestive	V↓ P↑ K↑
Lime	Sour	Cooling	Sweet	Refreshing, Digestive	V↓ P↓↑ K↑
Mango, green	Sour, Astringent	Cooling	Pungent	Heavy, Hard	V↑↓ P↑ K↓↑
Mango, ripe	Sweet	Heating	Sweet	Energizer	V↓ P↑↓ K↓↑
Melons	Sweet	Cooling	Sweet	Heavy, Hydrophilic	V↓ P↓ K↑
Oranges	Sweet, Sour	Heating	Pungent	Heavy	V↓ P↑ K↓↑
Papaya	Sweet, Sour	Heating	Sweet	Heavy, Unctuous	V↓ P↑ K↓↑
Peaches	Sour, Sweet, Astringent	Heating	Sweet	Heavy, Liquid	V↓ P↑ K↓
Pears	Sweet, Astringent	Cooling	Pungent	Dry, Rough, Heavy	V↑ P↓ K↓
Persimmon	Astringent, Sour	Heating	Pungent	Light, Dry, Sharp	V↑ P↓ K↓
Pineapple	Sweet, Sour	Heating	Sweet	Heavy, Sharp	V↓ P↑ K↓↑
Plums	Sweet, Sour, Astringent	Heating	Sweet	Heavy, Watery	V↓ P↑ K↑
Pomegranate	Sweet, Sour, Astringent	Cooling	Sweet	Smooth, Oily	V↓ P↓ K↓
Prunes, soaked	Sweet	Cooling	Sweet	Soothing, Laxative	V↓ P↓ K↓
Raisins, soaked	Sweet, Sour	Cooling	Sweet	Soothing, Laxative	V↓ P↓ K↓
Raisins, unsoaked	Sour	Cooling	Sweet	Light	V↑ P↓ K↓
Raspberries	Sweet, Sour, Astringent	Cooling	Pungent	Diuretic	V↑ P↓↑ K↓

FOOD	RASA	VIRYA	VIPAKA	ACTION ON DOSHA			
Rhubarb	Sweet	Heating	Sweet	Laxative, Heavy	V↓	P↑	K↑
Strawberries	Sour, Sweet, Astringent	Cooling	Pungent	Laxative, Urinary alkaline	V↑	P↓↑	K↓↑
Tamarind	Sour	Heating	Sour	Heating	V↓	P↑	K↑
Watermelon	Sweet	Cooling	Sweet	Heavy	V↑	P↓	K↑
VEGETABLES							
Artichoke	Astringent, Sweet	Heating	Sweet	Diuretic	V↑	P↓	K↓
Artichoke, Jerusalem	Astringent, Bitter	Cooling	Pungent	Light, Dry, Rough	V↑	P↓	K↓
Asparagus	Sweet, Astringent	Cooling	Sweet	Soothing, Tridoshic	V↓	P↓	K↓
Beets	Sweet	Cooling	Pungent	Heavy	V↑	P↑	K↓
Beet Greens	Astringent, Sweet	Cooling	Pungent	Light	V↑	P↓	K↓
Bitter Melon	Bitter	Cooling	Pungent	Diuretic, Regulates Blood Sugar	V↑	P↓	K↓
Broccoli	Astringent	Cooling	Pungent	Dry, Rough	V↑	P↓	K↓
Brussels Sprouts	Astringent	Heating	Pungent	Light, Diuretic	V↑	P↓	K↓
Burdock Root	Astringent, Bitter	Heating	Pungent	Light, Sharp, Diuretic	V↓	P↑	K↓
Cabbage	Astringent	Cooling	Pungent	Dry, Rough	V↑	P↓	K↓
Carrot, Raw	Astringent	Heating	Pungent	Hard, Rough, Heavy	V↑	P↑	K↓
Carrot, Cooked	Sweet	Heating	Pungent	Light, Soft	V↓	P↓↑	K↓
Cauliflower	Astringent	Cooling	Pungent	Dry, Rough	V↑	P↓	K↓
Celery	Astringent	Cooling	Pungent	Dry, Rough, Light	V↑	P↓	K↓
Chillies	Pungent	Heating	Pungent	Sharp, Hot	V↓	P↑	K↓
Cilantro	Sweet, Astringent	Cooling	Sweet	Delicate	V↓	P↓	K↓
Corn, fresh	Astringent, Sweet	Heating	Pungent	Light, Dry, Rough	V↑	P↑	K↓
Cucumber	Sweet	Cooling	Sweet	Soft, Liquid	V↓	P↓	K↑
Dandelion Greens	Bitter	Heating	Pungent	Light, Diuretic	V↑	P↓	K↓
Eggplant	Astringent, Bitter	Heating	Pungent	Heavy to digest	V↑	P↑	K↓
Fennel, fresh	Sweet, Sour	Cooling	Sweet	Laxative, Diuretic	V↓	P↓	K↓
Green Beans	Sweet, Astringent	Cooling	Pungent	Light	V↓	P↓	K↓
Kale	Bitter, Astringent	Cooling	Sweet	Dry, Rough	V↑	P↓	K↓
Kohlrabi	Astringent, Pungent	Heating	Pungent	Sharp, Diuretic, Light	V↑	P↑	K↓
Leeks, Cooked	Pungent, Sweet	Heating	Sweet	Stimulant	V↓	P↓	K↓
Lettuce	Astringent	Cooling	Pungent	Light, Liquid, Rough	V↑	P↓	K↓
Mushrooms	Astringent, Sweet	Heating	Pungent	Dry, Heavy, Slow	V↑	P↓	K↓
Mustard Greens	Pungent	Heating	Pungent	Sharp, Unctuous	V↓	P↑	K↓
Okra	Sweet, Astringent	Cooling	Sweet	Pod: Dry Rough; Seeds: Slimy if cooked	V↓	P↓	K↓
Olives (Black)	Sweet	Heating	Sweet	Heavy, Unctuous	V↓	P↑	K↑
Onion, cooked	Sweet, Pungent	Heating	Sweet	Digestive, Carminative	V↓	P↑↓	K↓
Onion, raw	Pungent	Heating	Pungent	Heavy, Appetizing	V↑	P↑	K↓

FOOD	RASA	VIRYA	VIPAKA	ACTION ON DOSHA			
Parsnip	Sweet, Astringent	Cooling	Sweet	Heavy Unctuous	V↓	P↓	K↑
Peas	Astringent	Cooling	Pungent	Hard, Slow, Heavy	V↑	P↓	K↓
Peppers	Sweet, Astringent	Heating	Sweet	Dry, Light, Stimulant	V↑	P↓	K↓
Potato, sweet	Sweet	Cooling	Sweet	Soft, Heavy	V↓	P↓	K↑
Potato, white	Astringent	Cooling	Sweet	Dry, Light, Rough	V↑	P↓	K↓
Radish	Pungent	Heating	Pungent	Hard, Liquid, Rough	V↑	P↑	K↓
Rutabaga	Astringent, Sweet	Cooling	Sweet	Heavy, Unctuous	V↓	P↓	K↑
Spinach, Raw	Astringent, Pungent	Cooling	Pungent	Dry, Light, Rough	V↑	P↓	K↓
Spinach, Cooked	Astringent, Sour	Heating	Sweet	Heavy, Laxative	V↓	P↑	K↓
Sprouts	Astringent	Cooling	Pungent	Light, Juicy	V↑	P↓	K↓
Squash, Winter	Astringent, Sweet	Heating	Pungent	Dry, Sharp, Heavy	V↑	P↑	K↓
Squash, Summer	Sweet, Astringent	Cooling	Pungent	Liquid, Heavy	V↓	P↓	K↑
Tomato	Sour, Sweet	Heating	Pungent	Nightshade, Disturbs doshas	V↑	P↑	K↑
Turnips	Pungent, Astringent	Heating	Pungent	Rough, Dry	V↑	P↑	K↓
Zucchini	Astringent	Cooling	Pungent	Heavy, Liquid	V↓	P↓	K↑
SWEETENERS							
Barley Malt	Sweet	Cooling	Sweet	Unctuous, Liquid	V↓	P↓	K↑
Date Sugar	Sweet	Cooling	Sweet	Heavy, Energizer, Oily	V↓	P↓	K↑
Fructose	Sweet	Cooling	Sweet	Unctuous, Liquid	V↓	P↓	K↑
Honey	Sweet	Heating	Sweet	Heating, Scrapes Fat	V↓	P↑	K↓
Jaggery	Sweet	Heating	Sweet	Strengthening, Heavy	V↓	P↑	K↑
Maple Syrup	Sweet	Cooling	Sweet	Light, Strengthener	V↓	P↓	K↑
Molasses	Sweet	Heating	Sweet	Heavy, Promotes bleeding	V↓	P↑	K↑
Rice Syrup	Sweet	Cooling	Sweet	Unctuous, Liquid	V↓	P↓	K↑
Sucanat	Sweet	Cooling	Sweet	Unctuous, Heavy	V↓	P↓	K↑
Sugar, white	Sweet	Cooling	Sweet	Heavy, Oily Energizer	V↑	P↓	K↑
Turbinado	Sweet	Cooling	Sweet	Unctuous	V↓	P↓	K↑
GRAINS							
Amaranth	Sweet, Astringent	Cooling	Pungent	Light	V↓	P↓	K↑
Barley	Sweet	Cooling	Sweet	Light, Diuretic	V↑	P↓	K↓
Buckwheat	Astring., Sweet, Pungent	Heating	Sweet	Heavy	V↑↓	P↑	K↓
Corn	Sweet	Heating	Sweet	Dry, Light	V↑	P↑	K↓
Durham Flour	Sweet, Astringent	Cooling	Sweet	Light	V↓	P↓	K↑
Millet	Sweet	Heating	Sweet	Dry, Light	V↑	P↑	K↓
Oat Bran	Astringent, Sweet	Cooling	Sweet	Rough, Dry, Light	V↑	P↓	K↓
Oats, dry	Sweet	Cooling	Sweet	Dry, Rough	V↑	P↓	K↓

FOOD	RASA	VIRYA	VIPAKA	ACTION ON DOSHA	V	P	K
Oats, cooked	Sweet	Cooling	Sweet	Heavy	V↓	P↓	K↑
Pasta (wheat)	Astringent	Cooling	Sweet	Heavy, Soft	V↑	P↓	K↑
Quinoa	Sweet, Astringent	Cooling	Sweet	Grounding	V↓	P↓	K↓↑
Rice, Basmati	Sweet	Cooling	Sweet	Light, Soft, Wholesome	V↓	P↓	K↑
Rice, Brown	Sweet	Heating	Sweet	Heavy	V↓	P↑	K↑
Rice Cakes	Astringent, Sweet	Cooling	Sweet	Drying, Light	V↓	P↓	K↓
Rice, White	Sweet	Cooling	Sweet	Holds water, Soft	V↓	P↓	K↑
Rye	Astringent	Heating	Pungent	Dry, Light	V↑	P↑	K↓
Sago	Astringent, Sweet	Cooling	Sweet	Drying, Light	V↓	P↓	K↓
Seitan	Sweet	Heating	Sweet	Heating, Light	V↓	P↓	K↓
Spelt	Pungent, Astringent	Heating	Pungent	Light, Dry	V↑	P↑	K↑
Tapioca	Astringent, Sweet	Cooling	Sweet	Drying, Light	V↑	P↓	K↓
Wheat	Sweet	Cooling	Sweet	Heavy, Unctuous, Laxative	V↓	P↓	K↑
LEGUMES							
Aduki	Astringent	Cooling	Pungent	Hard, Heavy	V↑	P↓	K↓
Black-Eyed Peas	Astringent	Cooling	Pungent	Hard, Heavy	V↑	P↓	K↓
Garbanzo (Chick Peas)	Sweet	Cooling	Pungent	Dry, Rough, Heavy	V↑	P↓	K↑
Kidney Beans	Astringent	Heating	Pungent	Hard, Rough, Heavy	V↓	P↑	K↑
Lentil, Brown	Astringent	Heating	Pungent	Rough, Heavy	V↑	P↑ K↓	
Lentil, Red	Sweet, Astringent	Cooling	Sweet	Light, Soft	V↑	P↓	K↓
Miso	Astringent, Sour	Heating	Pungent	Fermented	V↓	P↑	K↑
Mung Beans	Sweet, Astringent	Cooling	Sweet	Light, dry	V↓	P↓	K↓↑
Navy Beans	Sweet, Astringent	Heating	Pungent	Dry, Rough	V↑	P↓	K↓
Pinto Beans	Astringent	Cooling	Pungent	Hard to Digest	V↑	P↓	K↓
Soy Beans	Astringent, Sweet	Cooling	Pungent	Unctuous, Heavy	V↑	P↓	K↑
Soy Cheese	Astringent, Sour	Heating	Pungent	Heavy	V↓	P↑	K↑
Soy Sauce	Astringent, Sour	Heating	Pungent		V↓	P↑	K↑
Soy Sausages	Astringent, Sour	Heating	Pungent	Fermented	V↑	P↑	K↑
Soy Flour & Powder	Astringent, Sour	Cooling	Pungent		V↑	P↓	K↑
Tempeh	Astringent	Heating	Pungent	Light	V↑	P↓	K↓
Tofu	Sweet, Astringent	Cooling	Pungent		V↑↓ P↓		K↓↑
Tur Dal	Astringent	Heating	Pungent	Hard, Heavy	V↓	P↑	K↑
Urad Dal	Sweet	Heating	Sweet	Heavy, Soft, Unctuous	V↓	P↑	K↑
White Beans	Astringent	Cooling	Pungent	Hard to Digest	V↑	P↓	K↓
DAIRY							
Butter	Sour	Heating	Pungent	Light, Binds the stool	V↓	P↓	K↑

FOOD	RASA	VIRYA	VIPAKA	ACTION ON DOSHA	V	P	K
Buttermilk	Sweet, Sour, Astringent	Cooling	Sweet	Heavy, Unctuous, Binding	V↓	P↑	K↑
Cheese, Hard	Sour	Heating	Sour	Heavy, Oily, Congestive	V↓	P↑	K↑
Cheese, Soft	Sour	Heating	Sour	Heavy, Unctuous	V↓	P↓	K↑
Cottage Cheese	Sour, Salty	Heating	Pungent	Lighter, less Heating	V↓	P↓	K↓
Cow's Milk	Sweet	Cooling	Sweet	Laxative, Heavy, Mucous ↑	V↓	P↓	K↑
Ghee	Sweet	Cooling	Sweet	Kindles Agni, Digestive	V↓	P↓	K↑
Goat's Milk	Sweet	Cooling	Pungent	Light, Strengthens, Mucous ↑	V↓	P↓	K↑
Sour Cream	Sour	Heating	Pungent	Heavy, Unctuous	V↓	P↑	K↑
Yogurt: fresh	Sweet, Sour	Cooling	Sweet	Hydrophilic, Mucous ↑	V↓	P↓	K↑
Yogurt: old/store bought	Sour	Heating	Pungent	Hydrophilic, Mucous ↑	V↓	P↑	K↑
ANIMAL FOODS							
Beef	Sweet	Heating	Sweet	Heavy, Thick	V↓	P↑	K↑
Buffalo	Sweet	Cooling	Sweet	Heavy, Dull	V↓	P↓	K↑
Chicken, Light	Astringent, Sweet	Heating	Sweet	Light, Unctuous	V↑	P↓	K↓
Chicken, Dark	Sweet	Heating	Sweet	Heavy, Heating	V↓	P↑	K↑
Duck	Sweet, Pungent	Heating	Sweet	Heating, Heavy	V↓	P↑	K↑
Eggs	Sweet	Heating	Sweet	Unctuous, Heavy	V↓	P↑	K↓↑
Eggs, Yolk	Sweet	Heating	Sweet	Cholesterol ↑	V↓	P↑	K↑
Eggs, White	Sweet	Heating	Sweet		V↓	P↓	K↓
Fish, Freshwater	Sweet, Astringent	Heating	Sweet	Light, Unctuous, Soft	V↓	P↑	K↓↑
Fish, Salmon	Sweet	Heating	Sweet	Unctuous, Heating	V↓	P↑	K↑
Fish, Sea	Salty	Heating	Sweet		V↓	P↑	K↑
Fish, Tuna	Sweet, Salty, Astringent	Heating	Pungent	Heating	V↓	P↑	K↑
Lamb & Mutton	Sweet	Heating	Sweet	Strengthening, Heavy	V↑	P↑	K↑
Pork	Sweet	Heating	Sweet	Heavy, Unctuous	V↑	P↑	K↑
Rabbit	Sweet	Cooling	Pungent	Dry, Rough, Astringent	V↑	P↓	K↓
Shrimp	Sweet	Heating	Pungent	Light, Unctuous	V↓	P↑↓	K↓
Turkey, White	Sweet, Astringent	Cooling	Pungent		V↑	P↓	K↓
Turkey, Dark	Sweet, Astringent	Cooling	Pungent		V↓	P↑	K↑
Venison	Astringent	Cooling	Pungent	Light, Dry, Rough	V↑	P↓	K↓
NUTS							
Almond (w/ skin)	Sweet	Heating	Sweet	Oily, Heavy, Energizer	V↓	P↑	K↑
Almond (soaked peeled)	Sweet	Cooling	Sweet	Same as above	V↓	P↓	K↑
Brazil	Astringent, Sweet	Heating	Sweet	Unctuous	V↓	P↑	K↑
Cashew	Sweet	Heating	Sweet	Oily, Heavy, Energizer	V↓	P↑	K↑
Charoli	Sweet	Heating	Sweet	Delicate, Gentle	V↓	P↓	K↓

FOOD	RASA	VIRYA	VIPAKA	ACTION ON DOSHA	V P K
Coconut	Sweet	Cooling	Sweet	Helps mucous secretion	V↓ P↓ K↓
Hazelnut	Astringent, Sweet	Heating	Sweet	Energizes	V↓ P↑ K↑
Macadamia	Astringent, Sweet	Heating	Sweet	Energizes	V↓ P↑ K↑
Peanut	Sweet	Heating	Sweet	Oily, Heavy, Strengthens	V↓ P↑ K↑
Pecan	Astringent, Sweet	Heating	Sweet	Oily, Heavy	V↓ P↑ K↑
Pine nut	Astringent, Sweet	Heating	Sweet	Very Energizing	V↓ P↑ K↑
Pistachio	Sweet	Heating	Sweet	Oily, Energizer	V↓ P↑ K↑
Walnut	Sweet	Heating	Sweet	Oily, Heavy, Energizer	V↓ P↑ K↑
SEEDS					
Popcorn	Astringent, Sweet	Cooling	Pungent	Dry, Light, Rough	V↑ P↓ K↓
Psyllium	Astringent	Cooling	Pungent	Dry, Light, Rough	V↓ P↓ K↓
Pumpkin	Sweet	Heating	Pungent	Oily, Heavy, Hard	V↓ P↑↓ K↓
Safflower	Sweet, Astringent	Cooling	Sweet	Oily, Light, Soft	V↓ P↓ K↓
Sesame	Sweet, Bitter, Astringent	Heating	Pungent	Oily, Heavy, Smooth	V↓ P↑ K↑
Sunflower	Sweet, Astringent	Cooling	Sweet	Oily, Light, Soft	V↓ P↓ K↓
Kapha should use oils in very small amounts.					
OILS					
Almond	Sweet	Heating	Sweet	Heavy	V↓ P↑ K↑
Avocado	Sweet	Cooling	Sweet	Unctuous, Sweet	V↓ P↓ K↑
Castor oil	Sweet, Bitter	Heating	Sweet	Heavy, Cools External, Heats Internal	V↓ P↓ K↑
Coconut	Sweet	Cooling	Sweet	Unctuous, Heavy	V↓ P↓ K↑
Corn	Sweet, Astringent	Heating	Pungent	Dry, Rough, Heating	V↑ P↑ K↓
Canola	Astringent	Cooling	Pungent	Dry, Rough, Light	V↑ P↓ K↓
Ghee	Sweet	Cooling	Sweet	Heavy, Kindles Agni	V↓ P↓ K↓↑
Mustard	Pungent	Heating	Pungent	Sharp, Strong-smelling	V↓ P↑ K↓
Olive	Sweet	Cooling	Sweet	Heavy, Causes cellulite	V↓ P↓ K↑
Peanut	Sweet	Heating	Sweet	Strengthening	V↓ P↑ K↑
Safflower	Sweet, Astringent	Heating	Pungent	Light, Sharp, Oily	V↓ P↑ K↑
Sesame	Sweet, Bitter	Heating	Sweet	Strengthens, Lubricates	V↓ P↑ K↑
Soy	Astringent	Cooling	Pungent	Dry, Rough, Heavy	V↑ P↓ K↑
Sunflower	Sweet, Astringent	Cooling	Sweet	Soothing, Lubricating	V↓ P↓ K↓
SPICES					
Ajwan	Pungent	Heating	Pungent	Sharp, Light, Digestive	V↓ P↑ K↓
Allspice	Pungent	Heating	Pungent	Agni ↑ liquefies Kapha	V↓ P↑ K↓
Anise	Pungent	Heating	Pungent	Light, Detoxifying	V↓ P↑ K↓
Basil	Sweet, Pungent, Astring.	Heating	Pungent	Diaphoretic	V↓ P↑ K↓

FOOD	RASA	VIRYA	VIPAKA	ACTION ON DOSHA	V	P	K
Bay Leaf	Sweet, Pungent, Astring.	Heating	Pungent	Diaphoretic	V↓	P↑	K↓
Black Pepper	Pungent	Heating	Pungent	Dry, Sharp, Digestive	V↓	P↑	K↓
Caraway	Sweet, Astringent	Cooling	Pungent	Stimulates Agni	V↓	P↓	K↓
Cardamom	Sweet, Pungent	Heating	Sweet	Light, Oily, Digestive	V↓	P↑↓	K↓
Cayenne	Pungent	Heating	Pungent	Hot, Dry	V↑	P↑	K↓
Chocolate	Sweet, Bitter	Heating	Sweet	Hyperactive, Acidic, Congests	V↓	P↑↓	K↓
Cinnamon	Sweet, Pungent	Heating	Pungent	Dry, Light, Oily	V↓	P↑↓	K↓
Clove	Pungent	Heating	Sweet	Light, Oily	V↓	P↑	K↓
Coriander	Sweet, Astringent	Cooling	Sweet	Light, Oily, Smooth	V↓	P↓	K↓
Cumin	Pungent, Bitter	Cooling	Pungent	Digestive	V↓	P↓	K↓
Dill	Bitter, Astringent	Heating	Pungent	Light, Antispasmodic	V↓	P↑↓	K↓
Fennel	Sweet, Astringent	Cooling	Sweet	Delicate, Laxative	V↓	P↓	K↓
Fenugreek	Pungent, Bitter	Heating	Pungent	Kindles Agni	V↓	P↑	K↓
Garlic	All tastes except salty	Heating	Pungent	Oily, Heavy	V↓	P↑	K↓
Ginger, Dry	Pungent	Heating	Pungent	Light, Digestive	V↓	P↑	K↓
Ginger, Fresh	Pungent	Heating	Sweet	Light, Juicy, Digestive	V↓	P↑↓	K↓
Horseradish	Pungent, Astringent	Heating	Pungent	Kindles Agni	V↓	P↑	K↓
Hing	Pungent	Heating	Pungent	Dry, Sharp, Digestive	V↓	P↑	K↓
Mace	Pungent, Astringent, Sour	Heating	Pungent	Kindles Agni	V↓	P↑	K↓
Marjoram	Pungent, Astringent	Heating	Pungent	Kindles Agni	V↓	P↑	K↓
Mint	Sweet	Cooling	Pungent	Calms Pitta	V↓	P↓	K↓
Mustard	Pungent	Heating	Pungent	Sharp, Oily, Light	V↓	P↑	K↓
Neem Leaves	Bitter	Cooling	Pungent	Stimulates V slightly	V↑↓	P↓	K↓
Nutmeg	Sweet, Astringent, Pungent	Heating	Pungent	Stimulates digestion	V↓	P↑	K↓
Oregano	Astringent, Pungent	Heating	Pungent	Digestive	V↓	P↑	K↓
Paprika	Pungent	Heating	Pungent	Stimulates Agni	V↓	P↑	K↓
Parsley	Astringent Pungent	Heating	Pungent	May Stimulate Pitta	V↓	P↑↓	K↓
Poppy Seed	Astringent, Sweet	Heating	Pungent	Binds Stool, Aids Sleep	V↓	P↑	K↓
Rosemary	Astringent, Sweet	Heating	Pungent		V↓	P↑	K↓
Rosewater	Sweet, Sour,	Cooling	Sweet		V↓	P↓	K↓
Rock Salt	Salty	Heating	Sweet		V↓	P↑	K↑
Sea Salt	Salty	Heating	Pungent	Heavy, Hydrophilic	V↓	P↑	K↑
Saffron	Sweet, Astringent, Bitter	Heating	Sweet	Dry, Light, Aphrodisiac	V↓	P↓	K↓
Savory	Sour, Pungent	Heating	Pungent	Kindles Agni	V↓	P↑↓	K↑
Tarragon	Sweet	Cooling	Sweet		V↓	P↓	K↑
Turmeric	Bitter, Pungent, Astring.	Heating	Pungent	Dry, Light, Digestive	V↓	P↓	K↓
Vanilla	Sweet, Astringent	Cooling	Pungent		V↓	P↓	K↓

Glossary

Agni The biological fire of digestion and metabolism providing energy for the body to function.

Ajwan Wild celery seeds from India used in cooking and as a medicinal herb. Especially good as a strong digestive.

Ama A general term for toxins within the body produced by poor metabolism. Bad food combining can be one of the factors.

Apana One of the five varieties of *vata*. Responsible for exhalation and excretion. Has a downward movement in the body.

Asafoetida See Hing.

Basmati Rice A long-grain scented rice originating in the foothills of the Himalayas in India. Very digestible and nutritious.

Bitter Melon An Indian vegetable also known as bitter gourd. It has distinctive wrinkled pale green skin and many medicinal uses.

Black Cumin Seed A spice seed from a wild relative of cumin. Grows extensively in Northern India. Often erroneously called black onion seed.

Cardamom Pods Pungent spice seed from a tropical plant. The black seeds inside the pods are usually ground and flavor desserts.

Chai General word for tea. Often refers to a spiced black tea made with milk and sugar.

Charole A small nut-like seed from India with a flavor like almonds. Often toasted. Used in desserts.

Chickpea Flour Also called gram flour. A finely-ground yellow flour made from roasted chana dal, a close relative to the chickpea.

Chutney A condiment made from fresh ingredients, such as cilantro or green or ripe mango. Sometimes served cooked and sometimes raw.

Cilantro Also called coriander leaf, this herb is used extensively in Indian cooking and valued for its zesty and cooling taste. The perfect balance for spicy dishes.

Curry Leaves A small, fragrant leaf from a wild plant in India. They are widely used and an important ingredient in curry powder. Best used fresh.

Daikon A large, long white radish, often used in Ayurvedic cooking.

Dal Any type of dried bean, pea or lentil is called dal. Most dal is husked and split for quick cooking and digestibility. Sometimes dal is oiled to help preserve it.

Dosha Literally means fault or blemish. *Dosha* refers to the three principles or forces—*vata, pitta* and *kapha*—that maintain the integrity of the human body.

Fenugreek A small seed from India that is actually a legume. Mostly dry roasted and used in curries, dals and pickles.

Food Combining A term used to discuss various food combinations and the ways that "good or bad" ones will be assimilated in the body.

Ghee A clarified oil made from unsalted butter that has been gently cooked, and the milk solids removed.

Gram See Chickpea Flour.

Hing A spice from the sun-dried sap of a large Indian plant related to fennel. Has a strong smell and is an excellent digestive, especially helps reduce gas caused by beans. Use in small quantities and use only the compound type sold on the market in tins (often under the Cobra Brand). Pure hing is too strong for cooking.

Jaggary An unrefined sugar, made from the juice of crushed sugar cane stalks.

Kapha One of the three principles or *tridosha* of the body. *Kapha* has the elements of water and earth in its make up.

Khir A general term used to describe any sweet pudding made with milk.

Kitchari A cooked mixture of rice and dal and spices that is easy to digest and high in protein. Often used as a nourishing food for a mono-fast.

Kledak Kapha One of the five kinds of *kapha* in the body. It is active in the stomach and breaks down and liquefies food particles.

Kokam A small, sour Indian fruit usually sold dried.

Lassi A refreshing drink made from yogurt, water and spices, often served at the end of the meal as a digestive. Can be sweet or salty.

Masala Powder Masala means spice. It commonly refers to a mixture of spices, used to flavor dishes. Garam Masala is from the Punjab region of India.

Mung Dal A small green bean that has been husked and split. Usually a medium yellow color. Easy to digest

Murmura Basmati rice that has been popped. Often used as the basis of snack foods.

Nightshade Common name for a large family of plants—such as tomatoes, potatoes, tobacco, petunias and belladonna—that have strong medicinal properties.

Ojas The superfine essence in the body that produces the aura, provides strength against disease and moves energy from mind to body. Can be seen in the body as luster, especially in the eyes.

Pachak Pitta One of the five subtypes of *pitta*. The digestive juice located between the stomach and duodenum.

Panchakarma The five methods of purification, used to rid the body of excess *doshas*.

Pickle Masala Powder A mixture of spices specifically for making pickles. Tends to be quite spicy and hot.

Pippali This spice is a close relative to black pepper and has many medicinal properties especially for digestion and respiration.

Pitta One of the three bodily humors or *doshas*. Sometimes referred to the bile principle.

Poha Basmati rice that has been pounded or rolled. Can be thick and made into a lunch dish, or thin and used in a snack food. Doesn't require much cooking.

Prabhav The taste action that occurs when a substance has an unexpected and unexplained action, such as honey (sweet) being heating rather than cooling.

Prakruti The inherent nature of a person. The fixed constitution—the proportion of the three *doshas*—established at conception.

Prana The life force, the vital energy that activates body and mind. Equivalent to the Chinese *chi*.

Rasa The first experience of a food in the mouth. The taste of food. There are six tastes—sweet, sour, salty, bitter, pungent and astringent.

Saffron This golden yellow spice comes from the stigma of a particular crocus. The best quality is grown in Spain and Kashmir and must be picked by hand. The unique flavor and color is prized.

Samana One of the subtypes of *vata*. Located in the stomach and duodenum. Important in the digestion of food.

Sucanat A granulated natural sugar made from pure sugar cane juice.

Tridosha The three body humors or principles of *vata, pitta* and *kapha* within the body.

Tulsi The sacred, holy Indian basil plant. Sacred plant of Krishna. It is said to open the heart and the mind, bestowing the energy of love and devotion.

Tur Dal A split lentil from a plant known as a pigeon pea in English.

Turbinado A granulated natural sugar made from pure sugar cane.

Turmeric Root An underground rhizome from a perennial plant native to southern India and Asia. Comes in a red and a yellow form, but only the yellow is eaten. Can be used fresh or dried. It is an essential ingredient in most recipes.

Urad Dal This dried bean is a close relative of the mung bean, creamy white inside with a blackish skin. Has a high protein content.

Vata One of the three bodily humors or *doshas* in the body. Often referred to as the air and space principle.

Vikruti The current state of one's body or well-being as different from one's *prakruti.*

Vipaka This is the taste action or the post-digestive effect of a food after it has undergone digestive and assimilative transformation. There are three types—Sweet, Sour and Pungent.

Virya The second experience of taste, when the food gets into the stomach and creates a sense of heat or cold.

Index

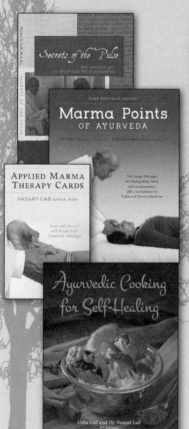

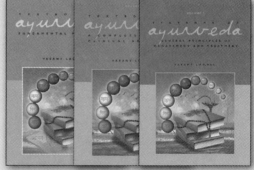